Harnessing the Trade Winds

The story of the centuries-old Indian trade with East Africa, using the Monsoon winds.

Photo: Blanche D' Souza

Sir Bartle Frere

Courtesy of Asiatic Society of Bombay

First published in Kenya in 2008 by Zand Graphics Ltd
Reprinted in India 2021 by Pentagon Press LLP

ISBN 978-93-90095-43-8

Published by PENTAGON PRESS LLP
206, Peacock Lane, Shahpur Jat, New Delhi-110049
Phones: 011-64706243, 26491568; Telefax: 011-26490600
email: rajan@pentagonpress.in; website: www.pentagonpress.in

Printed at Aegean Offset Printers, Greater Noida

Table of Contents

Acknowledgements

This monograph would not be complete without acknowledging the help, encouragement, goading if you like, of many of my friends and those who became friends through the writing of this book.

First and foremost I must acknowledge the help given me by the late Jayant Ruparel both moral and material, when I told him about my intention to write about the very early Indian trade with Africa he understood exactly what I was talking about. But he noticed that I was taking too long with my research, so one day he told me, "Just write, you will never complete your research. Later you can write a second edition." A true friend who took time off from his busy life to talk to me and bring relevant material from his personal collection to help in my research.

The second acknowledgement goes to a friend and colleague at the Library of Congress, also sadly departed, Najmu-Deen Durrani. Nazmi had a large collection of Africana which I used extensively in my research. His collection yielded so much useful information and formed the nucleus of what eventually became 'my book'.

I must also acknowledge the work done by the late Gaby de Souza, Cartographer. He did all the maps in my book. When my publisher saw his work he pronounced it 'a work of art'. Gaby was a quiet, perfectionist.

At the Xavier Centre of Historical Research in Goa, I introduced myself to Lilia Maria D'Souza, the bi-lingual (Portuguese/English) Librarian. She is not only efficient but takes a personal interest in the needs of the users of the library. She immediately understood what I was researching. I spent about ten days at the Centre and after the first two days I would find some books, manuscripts and other relevant material on 'my table' when I arrived. I am most grateful for this service, which lessened and lightened my 'search' time.

I am sure I have to thank many more people who took an interest in my writing although I must say not all understood the fervour that I felt towards writing the real story of our past in East Africa.

Blanche Rocha D'Souza.

Preface

History is of course written by the conquerors not the conquered
Dana April Seidenberg, 1996. In *Mercantile Adventurers*

This book records my journey to uncover the remarkable trade that existed between India and East Africa for at least three millennia - a phenomena that has thus far gone largely unmarked by historians.

After being away from Africa since the age of six I returned to Kenya in October 1951 on completion of my education in Karachi, British India. I started teaching at the Dr. Ribeiro Goan School, Nairobi in January 1952. Independence had come to India in 1947 and so, having lived a few years in independent Pakistan, I felt I was going back in time in colonial Kenya as regards discrimination by colour and race. I got to thinking about the history we had learnt in school. Freedom fighters were portrayed as troublemakers and traitors and believe it or not, our young minds actually thought so!

About this time the Mau Mau freedom movement was gaining momentum in Kenya. My parents lived in Nyeri 'in the thick of it' one might say. On one of my trips home for the holidays I heard that Mr. Gama Pinto who worked for the Colonial Administration in Nyeri, had a son Pio imprisoned by the British in Lamu in the Portuguese fort, because of his anti-British/pro-African sentiments. Pio was very ill at this time and his father, Mr Gama Pinto was asked to make a trip to Lamu to tell his son that he would be released if he promised not to get involved in politics. I thought, as did many Indians that he would listen to his father! But one had to know Pio better. A very dejected Mr. Gama Pinto returned with Pio's answer. Luckily Pio recovered from his illness, in prison.

While shopping in Nairobi's Indian Bazaar like everyone else, I noticed that these *dukawallas* were no different from those I had encountered in Bohori Bazaar in Karachi. I wondered if they were related. Yes they were; they had come from the same country originally. Most of them spoke very poor English. How come? After having lived for so long in a British colony? But I discovered later that they were proud of their origin and their mother tongue. So when did they get here, how, why? One day I would find out.

I started my research at the Kenya National Archives where I had to pay a small fee for use of the library. The staff was efficient and helpful and allowed me to use the whole library. My first target was the Murumbi Collection. I found a wealth of information on my subject of interest. There were also box files containing pamphlets and manuscripts which revealed information on Asian political activities.

I then travelled to Zanzibar to the Zanzibar Archives. I was surprised to find how well preserved the library is, despite all the turmoil the Island has suffered. I had to return a second time to check information and this time I met Professor Abdul Sheriff. He was very helpful whenever I could not get photocopying done or encountered some other problem. He also selected some useful manuscripts for me.

My next destination was Mumbai, India. I had to make two trips to India as well. Both times I worked at the Asiatic Society Library where there is a fairly good collection of material on the historical period of 'Monsoon' trade between India and Africa. In Mumbai I also spent some very profitable time at the University of Mumbai, Kalina Campus, Jawaharlal Nehru Library. I had to plough through at least ten fully packed shelves to find information, but it was rewarding. Here I got information which I did not find anywhere else. I did not find many Indian authors and only a few Arab authors.

I also went to Goa and worked at the Xavier Centre of Historical Research. A great deal of literature is in Portuguese, but I gained a lot from the literature in English. This is a well stocked library on the Portuguese period in Africa and especially East Africa. The Librarian is bi-lingual so I had no language problem.

In all my research I found that Arab and particularly European sources of information downplayed the importance of Indian trade in the Indian Ocean which goes back at least three thousand years BC. *Harnessing the Trade Winds* attempts to kindle in the Indian diaspora a justifiable pride in the achievements of its forebears in East Africa, and indeed in other parts of the world, who helped the development of agriculture, industry and the globalization of trade, stemming from their trading activities in East Africa.

I have consistently used the term Indian for peoples of the Indian sub-continent of pre-independent India. These are the adventurers who ventured out of their homeland with trade goods, in search of trade. They are the true pioneers of trade and globalization and even though these early traders had no intention of settling in Africa, circumstances changed the course of their lives.

Blanche Rocha D'Souza

Foreword

While curating the Asian African Heritage Exhibition at the National Museums of Kenya (2000-2005) I particularly enjoyed reading the Visitor's Book. I remember one comment which read: 'I did not know Indians were important in Africa!' This comment amused me at first but later I realized how significant the remark is, because it is a reflection of how little the history of the Indian Ocean and Africa is known.

The overseas visitor's comment resonates with not only Africans but also Asian Africans. There is a vacuum in historical awareness about the formation of cultures and nations at the western rim of the Indian Ocean. This vacuum affects not only how Asian African communities view themselves but also the making of national identities in the East African regions emerging from colonialism.

Today there are a few Asian Africans, in fact only a handful, whose youth was spent in the era of the twin Indian sub-continental and East African freedom movements. They are the elders who carry the spirit of the time. Many of them adhere to an East African diaspora group which continues a vibrant discussion on racism and colonialism; rise of nationalism and black racism and their subsequent emigration from East Africa as undesirable citizens. Blanche D'Souza is an elder of this colonial-to-nationalist transition period. Her book *Harnessing the Trade Winds* is a testimony of a commitment to complete telling a story untold, or at best half told. Her story is an observation made from her life in British India and colonial Kenya.

Often I have encountered not only a general public but also academic opinion that African history is all Black and White. I remember a Kenyan historian, who was at the time also the Director of African Studies, dismissing the presence of Asians in East Africa as a 'historical accident'. By that he implied that it was a subject not deserving of a place in the history of Africa. This was at a public lecture filled to capacity at the University of Nairobi. The speaker was from the once renowned Department of History at the University of Nairobi. Apparently it was not in the interest of political correctness to give credit to the development, entrepreneurial skills - trade, architecture, horticulture and plantations of cloves, cotton and sugar - to a subject people of the mighty British raj or 'paper citizens' (versus 'blood citizens') of African nations.

Blanche D'Souza's book is a most direct statement on 'brown man's' transcripts over thousands of years of trade, labour and migrations for settlements against a pervading backdrop of Arab, British and Portuguese rivalries in the Indian Ocean. In this wake *Harnessing the Trade Winds* adds to plural historical perspectives, in that the text upholds the value of diversity that shapes the identities and self-knowledge of the peoples of Asia and Africa. It challenges those who hold the political reigns and direct policy, on education as well as race relations.

Harnessing the Trade Winds is an outcome of a generation of research undertaken in Nairobi, Mombasa and Zanzibar in East Africa and Mumbai and Goa in India.

Nearly half a century ago the author, Blanche D'Souza was my English teacher at a Catholic mission school in Nairobi. Her students remember her as Miss Blanche who challenged the authority of the Church run school to 'cane' children. She continues to live in Nairobi after raising a large family.

Sultan Somjee PhD
Curator, *The Asian African Heritage Exhibition 2000-2005,*
National Museums of Kenya

Introduction

Harnessing the Trade Winds

> **Globalization is not new nor is it just Westernization. Over thousands of years globalization has progressed through travel, trade, migration, spread of cultural influences and dissemination of knowledge and understanding (including of science and technology)**
> (Amartya Sen)

It is a common belief that the first Indians came to East Africa as railway construction workers, coolies with only the shirt on their backs along with the artisans, clerks, accountants and soldiers, and that the present Asian population are their descendants. In fact of the 32,000 Indians who were brought over with artisan and other skills to build the Uganda Railway in 1896, close to 16,312 returned to India (Ghai, 1990). At the time of the building of the railway there were already 13,000 Indians residing in East Africa. They were living and working there at least as long as the Arabs (Coupland, 1939). Allidina Visram for instance was in Uganda twenty years before the start of the railway with well established trading posts in all three East African territories. There were many others too, like Adamjee Alibhoy and M. G. Puri, with stable businesses.

Exploration of the eastern coast of Africa started earlier than travels on the western coast but it has less of a history. Traders from Arabia and India had been visiting the East African coast for millennia. By AD 1,000 there were established markets and settlements on the coast, these villages were the forerunners of the Swahili city states. By this time Indians were joined by peoples of Indonesia, Sumatra, Java, Malaya (Malaysia) and Borneo.

In 1498 Vasco da Gama and the other Europeans that followed him to Africa found a trade relative to the rest of the world, much bigger in fact and more important than thought at first, carried out in dhows. All this trade was in the hands of 'men whose homes were in India'.

Chapter 1

Trading links with Africa before recorded history

From earliest times the East African coast was involved in a network of trade carried on by merchant seamen from India, Persia and Arabia. Traders from northwest India were sailing to the African coast long before recorded history. Trade was carried out in Indian dhows down the coast of East Africa as far as Mozambique and back again down the west coast of India.

In Vedic times enterprising merchants sent ships to foreign lands in pursuit of gain, frequenting every part of the ocean. The Hindu Vedas (holy books) the most ancient Hindu scriptures, especially the collection of four Vedas or sacred knowledge, namely R*ig-Veda, Sama-Veda, Yajur-Veda* and *Atharva-Veda,* are older than the *Puranas*. The language of the Vedas is an older form of Sanskrit. All Vedic literature was not written at the same time. The Hindu *Rig-Veda,* the first of the four books of Vedic literature was written about 1,200 BC. The *Brahamanas* and *Upanishads* were written about 600 BC. The *Rig-Veda* the earliest literary work of the Indians or Indo-Aryans, records voyages, storms, shipwrecks and a sea borne trade with the ocean as a highway of commerce and communications.

The Vedas referred to a mysterious realm called Chandristan or 'Country of the Moon' where exist the Mountains of the Moon (Rwenzori) or Chandra Giri in which the Nile or Neel Ganga (Dark Ganges) has its source. They also seem to have made a distinction between the White Nile and the Blue Nile (Neel Ganga and Shvet Ganga), which they obviously had first hand knowledge about.

From the excavations at Harappa and Mohen-jo-Daro (2,500 BC-1,500 BC), the largest cities of the pre-historic Indus Valley civilization, monuments reveal that a sea borne trade existed with Mesopotamia from the Tigris and Euphrates Rivers to the western coast of India around 200 BC. According to Charles Vanderlinden:

> It seems that around 300 BC Indians from the Indus Valley had established maritime contact with Mesopotamia and Egypt. They must have had means of transporting heavy and cumbersome goods, for ruins show traces of Indian teak wood found in these areas dating back to that time. These early exploits were of Dravidians and later of Aryans according to Sanskrit and Pali texts. (Chandra, 1987).

Commercial relations between India and Africa sustained by private enterprise can be reliably traced to the age of the *Puranas* AD 300 to AD 700, Hindu sacred writings consisting of 18 *Puranas* in all, a collection of traditional lore, stories, epics, myths and legends.

When the explorer Speke landed in Zanzibar on 17th August 1860 on his search for the source of the Nile he met the British Consul who gave him a 'most interesting paper' with a map attached, which was to guide him in his quest for the source of the Nile. The paper was written by Lt. Francis Wilford and read to the Asiatic Society in Calcutta in 1792. The text was from the *Puranas* of the ancient Hindus concerning the source of the Nile which they called Krishna.

The third volume of the Asiatic Researhes of 1799 contains a paper giving information on the River Nile from an extract also taken from the *Puranas*. These early Hindus knew of a great sweet water lake (Lake Victoria) which they named Amar (immortal). Speke in his journal wrote:

> It is remarkable that the Hindus have christened the source of the Nile Amara which is a country at the northeast corner of Victoria Nyanza.

The modern view of the Amara River is a considerable stream flowing through the Maasai Mara Reserve of Kenya. This clearly shows that the ancient Hindus must have travelled widely to have had some communication with both the northern and southern ends of Deva Sarobara or Lake of the Gods, the Puranic name for Lake Victoria.

These Indians discovered the Monsoons, as they called the reliable Trade Winds of the Indian Ocean, which blow northeast towards Africa from November to March/April and back again southwest towards India from May to September/October. (Marsh, 1961).

The original inhabitants of India were Dravidians but by 2 BC Aryans from northwest Asia (Kazakhstan, Uzbekistan) began to infiltrate India through the passes in the Himalayas, becoming the predominant race in India.

There was great intensification of trade in AD 2 according to Ptolemy, caused by the demand in the Roman Empire for luxury goods brought via the Red Sea to Egypt, from India and Ceylon (Sri Lanka). Later there grew a flourishing trade with South East Asia, the Grecco-Roman world, the Near East, Persia and Central Asia, overland and by sea with East Africa, enriching India's culture, civilization and peoples of various races.

In Homburger's *Historical Conclusions from a Study of Indo-African Languages,* the first dynastic Egyptians came from the Indus Valley with the traders that preceded them. India maintained constant contact with the people of Egypt through trade, hence the two civilizations are identical.

India and Egypt are the cradles of the most ancient civilizations that flourished on the banks of the Indus and Nile Rivers. Egypt and the Red Sea or Bab-el-Mandeb (Sea of Lamentations) to the Arabs, the Arabian Gulf and Muscat were scenes of very early civilizations. The Red Sea leads up to Egypt and the Arabian Gulf leads up to Babylonia and Sumaria. In the *Ramayana* the Red Sea is called Lohita Sagar. The *Puranas* also mention Miair as ancient Egypt. Ivory, ebony and cotton goods were brought to Egypt in the 2nd century BC. Egyptian mummies were wrapped in Indian silk. This ancient commerce grew out of the the needs of the Pharaohs for spices, precious stones, sandalwood and the incense of India. Brisk trade between India and Egypt led to Indian settlement in Egypt and Egyptian settlement in India. An Egyptian scholar, El Manswori, has pointed out that both India and Egypt worship the cow, bull, sun, snake and river.

Claudius Ptolemy (AD 2), who wrote a geography book, was the first Greek to mention the Mountains of the Moon and connect them with the Nile. Ptolemy claims that he got his information regarding these mountains in Alexandria, from Brahmins of India. Speke supposes that the high group of hills near Lake Tanganyika were the *Lunae Montes* in Ptolemy's geography.

Reference has been made to the ancient trade carried on by the Phoenicians with Arabs and Hindus in Eastern Africa probably long before the joint expeditions which Hiran, King of Tyre on the Mediterranean, and Solomon King of Israel, sent from Ezion-Geber (Red Sea) as far as Madagascar. About the earliest definite hint of trade routes down the coast of East Africa is the passage in the Bible of ships of Solomon and Hiran, buying 'gold of Ophir' which exported large quantities of this commodity through the port of Sofala to Arabia, India and China. The Portuguese positively identified Sofala gold as coming from the 'Land of Ophir' (Zimbabwe) in Central Africa. King Solomon gave the Phoenicians a port on the Red Sea in order to open trade with the East, where Indians and Arabs had been trading on the East African coast long before this time (Stigand, 1966).

Since the time of the Pharaohs Europeans had participated in the Indian Ocean trade through Egypt, where the Venetians monopolized the Mediterranean Sea trade. A thriving commerce existed overland between southern India and the Roman Empire in the early centuries of the Christian era, as well as between India and Asia Minor, Syria, Egypt and East Africa. It is not known if Indians preceded the Arabs in this trade but it is clear that seafaring was common during the Buddhist era of Indian history (Gautama Buddha 563 BC-483 BC). Sanchi scriptures of 2 BC contain pictures of carvings of ships in East African coastal towns (Hailey, 1957). Indian Ocean trade is known to have taken place at least 500 BC, but the first Arab settlements on the East African coast date back to about AD 800.

India's trade relations with Ethiopia are almost as old as those with Egypt. The ancient kingdom of Ethiopia revolved around its capital Auxum. A written religious language Ge'ez was probably influenced by the Indian Brahmi and Kharoshti scripts through Indian traders who traded with Ethiopia and Egypt in the pre-Christian era. The Ethiopian system of vowels indicates Sanskrit influence. The importance of India's trade with the Auxumite Empire was highlighted by the discovery of 103 Kushana gold coins around AD 230.

Before the realization of the full potential of the Monsoon winds and the benefits of travel by sea, the bulk of the Indian trade to Egypt was carried on overland via the Sabean Lane, named after the Kingdom of Saba through which the overland trade passed to Egypt and the Mediterranean. The ancient Greeks called modern Yemen Saba or Sabea (170 BC to 100 BC), an area into which the Sabeans had moved after conquering Hadhramaut (an ancient southern Arabian kingdom that occupied southeast Yemen and present day Sultanate of Oman). Indian teak wood has been found in Yemen dating back to the 7th and 6th centuries BC (Gadre).

The rulers through whose territories the overland trade passed grew strong and wealthy on their control of the carrying trade between Asia and Africa. They held the Red Sea straits in their grip exacting dues from all those who passed through them in about 150 BC. A book on the Erythrean Sea (Indian Ocean) speaks of the wealth of the Sabeans in the southwest corner of Arabia. It is the first contemporary account of the commerce opened between India and Egypt through Arabia. In 177 BC the Greek sovereigns of Egypt did not trade directly with India but bought Indian goods from Saba or Sabea, imported through the port of present day Aden. Also, being placed in the line of commerce between Asia and Africa, Sabean kings of southern Arabia had exercised some rule over parts of the East African coast from the 1st century AD. However settlement on the African continent took place only in the 7th century AD when Sabeans from arid Arabia moved into the fertile mountains of Ethiopia (Stigand, 1913).

As far as the Empire of Kush (Sudan) is concerned scholars hold the view that the Indian Ocean trade entered Sudan through Egypt and the Mediterranean travelling up the White Nile River.

Record-keeping or recording history was not a practice of the early Indian traveller. Perhaps this was linked to the caste system where the trading caste not being the literate caste, was unable to write. Whereas the Brahmins who were literate, were not allowed to travel by sea or engage in trade. However they did travel by land, hence many geographical and historical discoveries were recorded in the *Puranas* or holy books of the ancient Hindus. Presumably they took the overland route through Yemen which Indian traders had been using for ages before sea travel became popular, to cross over the Red Sea to the East African coast. At a certain point at low tide, the Red Sea is only knee deep. This was the same crossing made by Moses in the Old Testament when he led the Israelites out of Egypt to the Promised Land.

There could also be another reason for lack of records. Hindu records were either perfunctory or the writing did not survive, because on the Malabar Coast writing was on fragile palm leaf sheets. (Hall, 1998).

No black African nation established itself as a sea-faring power. The absence of the spirit of adventure among the African nations of the past is historically significant. For if they had travelled to explore new lands, Africa would have had a very different past. Ancient Egyptians occasionally referred to the northeastern coast of Africa as 'Punt' connecting it with a civilization. The earliest black African civilization was probably in Punt, now Puntland, an autonomous state in northeast Somalia. Nevertheless, Sabeans from Yemen were the earliest important people whose settlement on the East African coast has been concretely proved. Trade in Arabian, Indian and East African products began under their rule. Eastern shipbuilding ideas and cultivated crops of Indian origin reached East Africa and North Africa, introduced by the Sabeans (Murdock, 1959).

There were a few settlements for trade and tropical agriculture in Roman times near the Equator, but nothing of significance. As the Roman

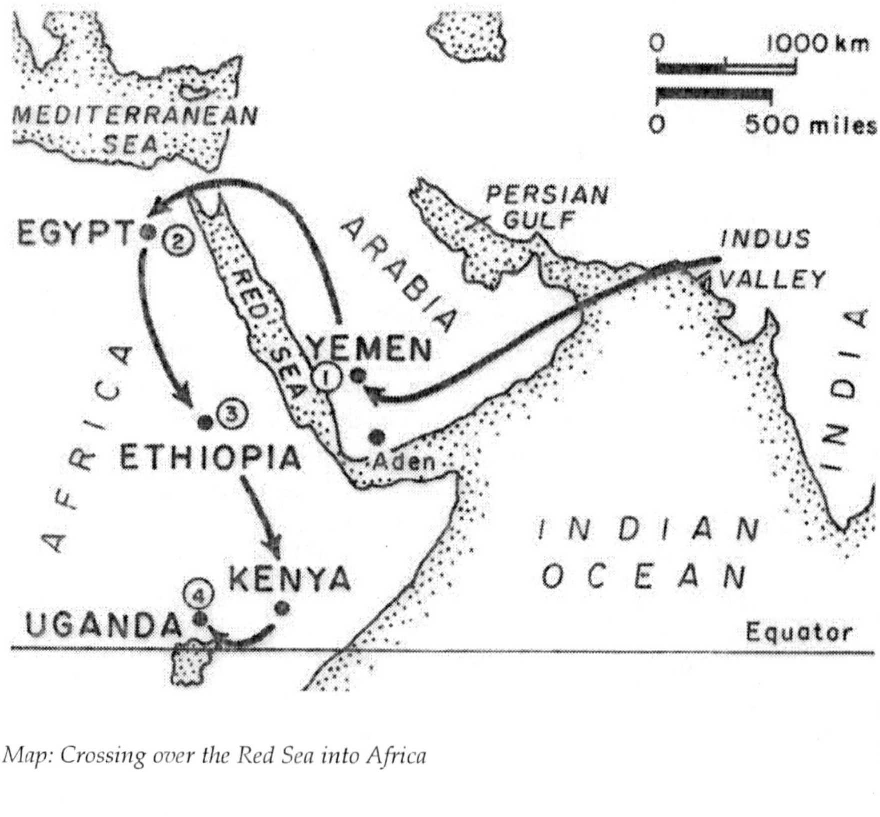

Map: Crossing over the Red Sea into Africa

Empire began to disintegrate in the 4th century AD, Romans and Greeks lost contact with India and Africa. (Trimizi, 1988).

There is every reason to believe that migration of peoples in prehistoric times took place both by land and sea. Colonial rulers and historians underplayed the role of non-Europeans in the growth of modern civilization.

Chapter 2

Early Indian Ocean Trade

Where India lay was but a hazy notion at this time. India included Southern Arabia, East Africa and even the East Indies. It would be more accurate to say that India was those lands whence came the costly products such as spices, aromatics and precious stones that were necessary for the comfort and adornment of the powerful and wealthy in Europe.
(Justus Strandes in *The Portuguese Period in East Africa,* 1961)

The history of the East African coast is to be studied as the history of the Indian Ocean. The culture and wealth on which its towns were founded came from eastern trade. Each town had its merchants, market place and port.

A great deal of work has been done to highlight India's trade before the coming of the Portuguese. In this trade India, because of its geographic position, sea and wind currents, availability and suitability of ports, size of internal markets and export potential, played a key role. Unfortunately through lack of record-keeping and a certain bent towards family secrecy on the part of the Indians, there is a notable absence of publicity. The Arabs were not the only adventurers on the Indian Ocean, for the same Trade Winds which proved so useful to them also carried the Indians to the East African coast. Arab sources therefore form the core information followed by Dutch, English and French, which can also be held responsible for any bias in recording.

The chief trade of India has always been with countries lying to the

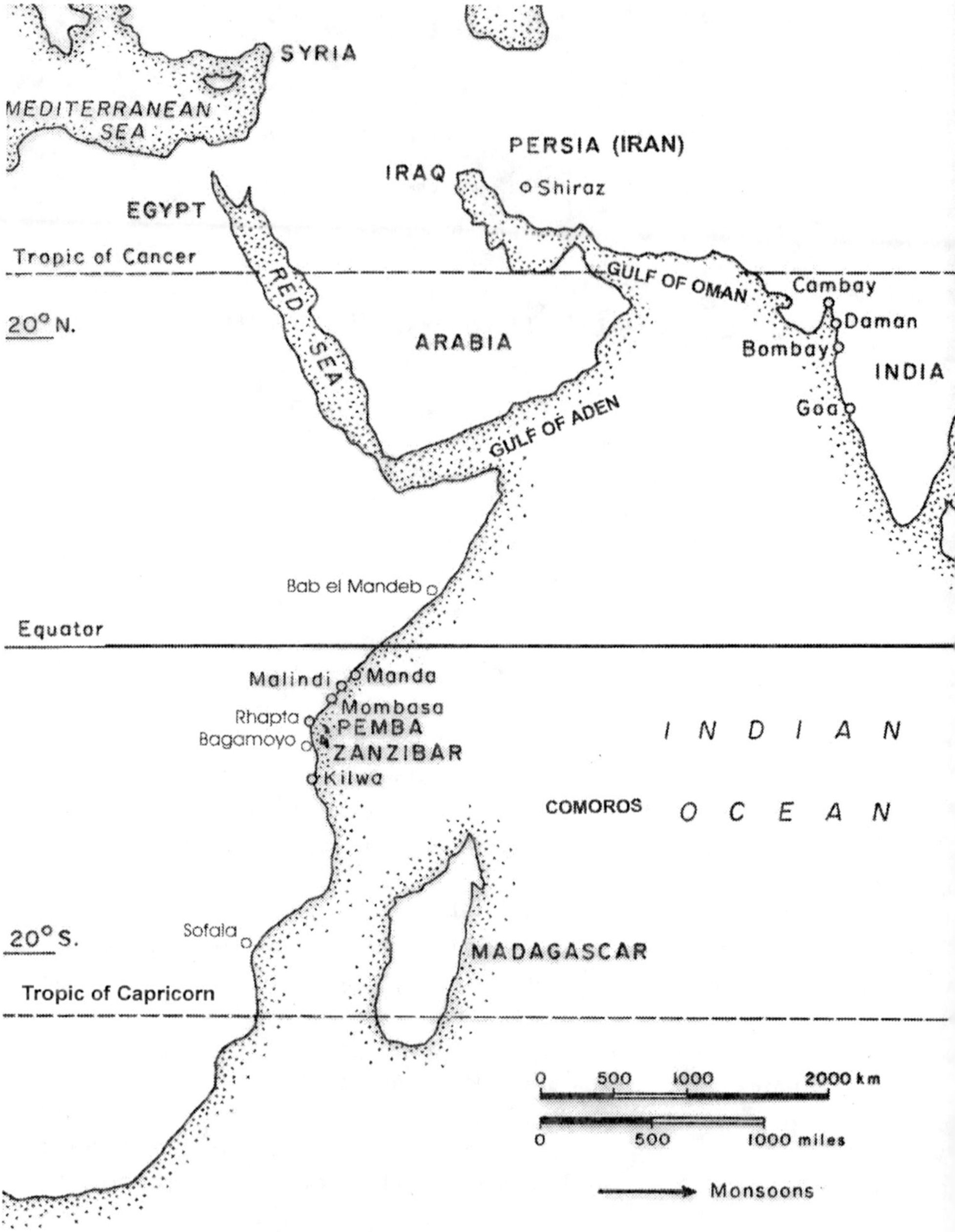

Map: Areas of early trade between India and East Africa
Source: African History by Philip Curtin, pg. 140

west, first over land and later by sea. In earliest times traffic passed through neighbouring states and by degrees a regular trade route was established between the Caspian Sea, Black Sea and the Indus by way of the Oxus River and the Hindu Kush, a mountain range in northeast Afghanistan. The difficulties of transporting goods of any bulk must have prevented this route from being used a lot, and eventually abandoned. However the overland trade route to the Red Sea via Saba or Sabea continued, becoming part of the commercial system linking the Mediterranean with the Middle East and East Africa, to the thriving markets of India.

Maritime activity on the Indian Ocean developed much earlier than it did on the Atlantic. Indian contact with the coastal region of Eastern Africa dates back many centuries Traders from India, Arabia and Persia had been visiting the East African coast since before the Iron Age, 1,000 BC (Kesby, 1977) in small sailing boats called dhows propelled by the Trade Winds. There is both written and archaeological evidence to show that trade between the west Indian and East African coasts flourished centuries before the advent of Europeans and that this trade was plied and controlled by Indians. The area covered was, the Straits of Bab el Mandeb on the North African coast, the islands of Pemba, Zanzibar, Comoros, Madagascar, the eastern shores of Arabia, western India and the Indonesian archipelago.

Sofala gold was the core of the trade and the trading nations were Yemen, India, Morocco and Spain. The Indian trading circuit included Egypt at one end and China at the other.

Alexander the Great (356-323 BC), King of Macedonia and a great traveller, reckoned that the Indian Ocean trade was directly linked to the Mediterranean through Egypt. Spices, rare woods and ivory were taken from India and Africa via the Red Sea and overland through Egypt to the Mediterranean countries. He also travelled extensively in India. A town in central India, Secunderabad, is named after Alexander the Great.

In 1154, al-Idris from the Mediterranean, recorded information concerning East Africa's most important export product to India, the highly prized iron ore. In 1340 Ibn al-Wardi, a geographer, tells of Sofala's deposits of iron ore, which were purer and more malleable than that mined in India. The Indians smelted the iron to produce steel for weapons and tools. In 1250 an inspector of customs in southern China, wrote about ships of the northwest kingdom of Gujerat that sailed every year to East

Africa, to the 'Land of Zanj' with supplies of cotton cloth and other goods.

From earliest times the East African coast was involved in a network of trade by merchant seamen from India, Persia and Arabia. Some time at the beginning of the 7th century BC, rice, sandalwood and peacocks were carried from India by sea to the Persian Gulf from India. The peacock rose to become Persia's national bird.

Trade with Africa started in the barter system. Food and cloth produced in India, for instance the 'shuka' for men, were bartered for African products. After a time millet was used as a monetary unit, and later Indian cowries were used as currency. An abundant source of cowries were the Maldives.

The first historical reference to Indian trade in the East African region is found in the *Periplus of the Erythrean Sea*, meaning 'Directory of the Indian Ocean'. It is a pilot's guide on sailing directions to the Indian Ocean, translated from Greek. The writer of this important nautical guide, probably a merchant mariner from Berenicke, a port on the Red Sea coast of Egypt, made a voyage round the Horn of Africa down the African coast to a market town named Rhapta, 'the last town of the Azania coast'.

Rhapta derived its name from the boats made of single planks 'sewn together with vegetable (coconut) fiber'. By the 4th century AD Rhapta was considered of great importance because of its exports of ivory and tortoise shell to India 'which trade was controlled by a ruler from Arabia'. The anonymous writer of the *Periplus* gives a brief description of the hazards and advantages of the East African run which took twenty-three days sailing from Ras Hafur just south of Guardafui down the Azanian coast, to Rhapta. By the time of Ptolemy's Geography AD 2, Rhapta was described as an important metropolis. The remnants of Rhapta have not been found but it is now positively thought to have been located on the Rufiji Delta in Tanganyika. (Stigand, 1913).

The writer of the *Periplus* further recounts the trade with Azania between his home harbours and northwestern India. The whole East African coast had been called Azania (place of intense heat) by the Greeks. Later it was known as the Land of 'Zanj' or 'Zenj', originally Persian, meaning the 'Land of the Blacks' once simply used to denote colour. He describes how as far back as AD 2, a flourishing trade existed in the Indian Ocean not only with Arabs but also with Indians, carried on in dhows from 'Ariake' (modern Konkan) and 'Barugaza' (modern Broach) bringing to the markets of East Africa 'products of their own place; wheat, rice,

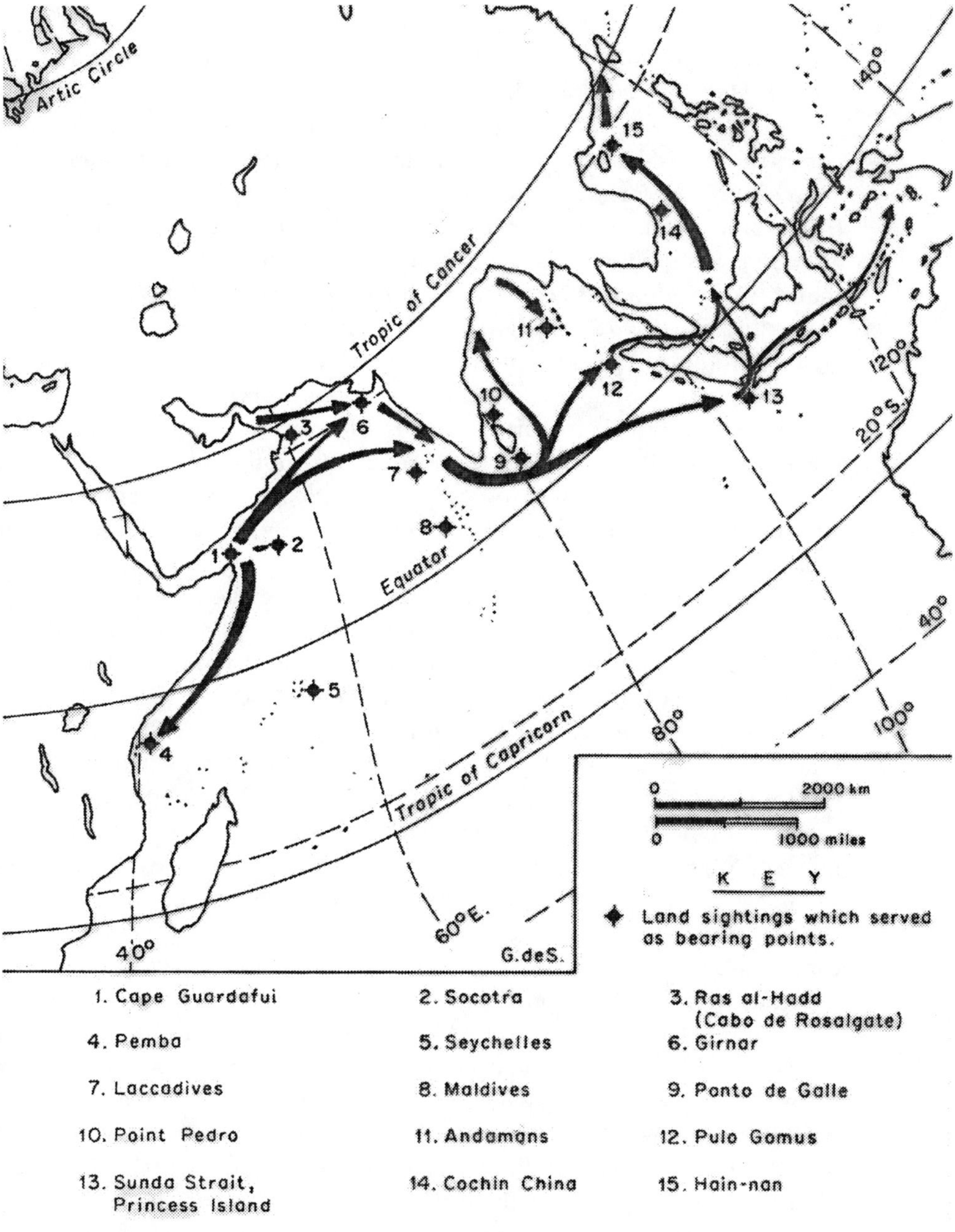

Map: The Main sea-lanes in the Indian Ocean
Source: History of Africa by Kevin Shillington, pg. 130

sesame oil, cotton cloth, metalware, glass and honey from a reed called 'sachari' (sugarcane). These were exchanged for ivory, rhinoceros horn, tortoise shell and coconut oil.

The Erythrean Sea (Indian Ocean) was considered by the Greeks to comprise the Red Sea, Persian Gulf and the Indian Ocean. Although it is an anonymous work, The *Periplus of the Erythrean Sea* has been accepted as the most authentic source of information regarding trade, commerce and geography as known in the 1st century AD. It is now unanimously agreed that it was written in AD 60. (East Africa Today, 1958-1959)

Pliny (AD 23-70), a Roman writer on geography in the 1st century AD, mentions in his famous book *Natural History* that cotton was an extremely rare product for any country except India, in ancient times. He calls it 'byssus' but clearly distinguishes it from hemp and flax. Cotton was found only in Mohen-jo-Daro (2,500-1,500 BC) in the Indus Valley. It was carried by the early traders to Egypt where it began to thrive in the fertile soil on the banks of the Nile River, to eventually become the best in the world.

Traders from northwest India were crossing the Indian Ocean long before recorded history. They came in small sailing boats called dhows. About AD 600 the Indian Ocean seemed studded with merchant ships. Arab ships made direct voyages to India and Ceylon (Sri Lanka) and further east to China. From the 6th to the 16th centuries the Arabs were masters of the Indian Ocean, aggressively carrying on their trade. While the Indians quietly but single-mindedly conducted their operations with their habitual trading centers, regularly crossing the Indian Ocean to the markets of East Africa, Malacca on the Malayan Peninsula, Java and Madagascar. They brought goods from the East to the Persian Gulf crossing the Red Sea to the African coast and from there overland on camelback through Egypt to the Mediterranean ports. Thus commercial relations between Asia and Europe began to flourish.

Abdul Hassan ibn Hussein Al-Masudi, an Omani Arab who sailed as far as Madagascar, was among the best informed travellers of the 'blind waters of the Sea of Zanj which was the most perilous of the world'. He wrote and travelled for 40 years. Although only two of his works, one being *Meadows of Gold*, are known they are unrivalled for early knowledge of the trading world especially the East African coast. In A.H. 304 (AD 916) he travelled to Persia, India and China and back again to Oman via East Africa.

On African trade he wrote:

> It is from this country that come tusks weighing fifty pounds and more. They go to Oman and from there are sent to China and India. They sail as far as Sofala, beyond that the Arabs did not go for once you entered the channel between Madagascar and Mozambique the Monsoon winds failed.

Whether from first hand information or from Arab sources early accounts of trade in Chinese books of the twelfth and thirteenth centuries mention the *Ta'shi* (Arab) people of *Ts'ong* (Zanzibar). Also that every year the *Hu-chi-u-la* (Gujerati) and the *Ta'shi* along the sea coast, send ships to China with products of their own country which include elephant tusks, native gold, ambergris, yellow sandalwood, white cotton cloth, porcelain and red pepper. Obviously this is a mixture of Indian and African products. The Chinese had established trading posts in southern India in the 12th century AD, but there is no evidence of Chinese sailors visiting East Africa at this time. Before the Ming Dynasty (AD 1368-1644) Chinese trade was carried on indirectly, using Indian ships. Although by the 12th century Chinese ships were technically capable of sailing anywhere, it was only in the 15th century that the famous Admiral Chung Ho made his first voyage to East Africa for trade. (Josephy, 1971)

The Venetian traveller Marco Polo (AD 1254-1324) travelled along both the east and west coasts of India. He was impressed with the riches of India especially Ceylon (Sri Lanka) which produced an abundance of rubies, sapphires and topazes. Along the Malabar Coast he saw pepper, cinnamon, ginger and other spices growing in abundance. He also wrote of trade relations between the Malabar coast of India and Zanzibar in the 13th century referring to Indian ships which visited the island of Madagascar and that other of 'Zanghibar'. This trade was centuries old even then. Marco Polo referred to Madagascar from hearsay for no European was known to have visited East Africa before the 15th century.

In 1270, when Marco Polo was on his way to Cathay (China) and Malabar in India, he stopped off at Hormuz (Ormuz), an ancient trading center at the mouth of the Persian Gulf where he had his first glimpse of the Indian Ocean, but he never sailed on it. He took an overland route to

China, the 'sewn boats' were too fragile for him. Two centuries later Vasco da Gama confirmed India's long established trade with the East African coast.

Indian ships traded with Egypt through the Red Sea, which was then a province of Rome. They sailed to all ports down the East African coast in the month of July to collect native products from the interior of Africa. Tomé Pirès, a Portuguese sailor who lived in Malacca, Malaysia (1512-1515), wrote of trade relations with India, Arabia and the Far East:

> People come to trade in these parts from many places, from Cambay, from the whole of Africa but chiefly from the City of Aden where Indians had an important trading port. They bring course cloths of many kinds, glass beads and other beads from Cambay. From Aden they bring raisins and from Ormuz dates. And they take away gold, ivory and slaves and trade them in the Ports of Zeila and Berbera. Goods are brought from Kilwa, Melindi, Brava, Mogadishu and Mombasa for the good horses of this Arabia. This trade is carried out by ships from Aden and Cambay, many of one and many of the other.

Goa was the centre for the trade in horses from Persia and Arabia (Salvadori, 1996).

> Yet was India that remained for East Africa the most important market and supplier. Indian beads became valuable as early as the 8th century; Indian textiles were brought into East African ports through centuries. As supplier of goods to Africa and consumer of goods from Africa the rising civilizations of west and south India would act on Africa for many hundreds of years. In India ivory was in demand for sword hilts, dagger hilts and chessmen. Gold was another. Large quantities of gold went to India

> from Africa adding to the glittering piles looted by Europeans after 1500. Iron, ivory and slaves, although slaves were a subsidiary compared to those bought by western countries. (Davidson, 1959).

The history of commerce is strewn with trails with exotic connotations. The Silk Road, the Spice Road, the Gold Road, the Salt Road. Salt was the most important commodity of the African trade, as common a medium as gold and the principal source was the Sahara Desert. The Silk Road was named by the Romans for the silk (serco) that came up the Red Sea through Egypt.

Thus East Africa had gained its place in the network of trade through Arab and Indian efforts.

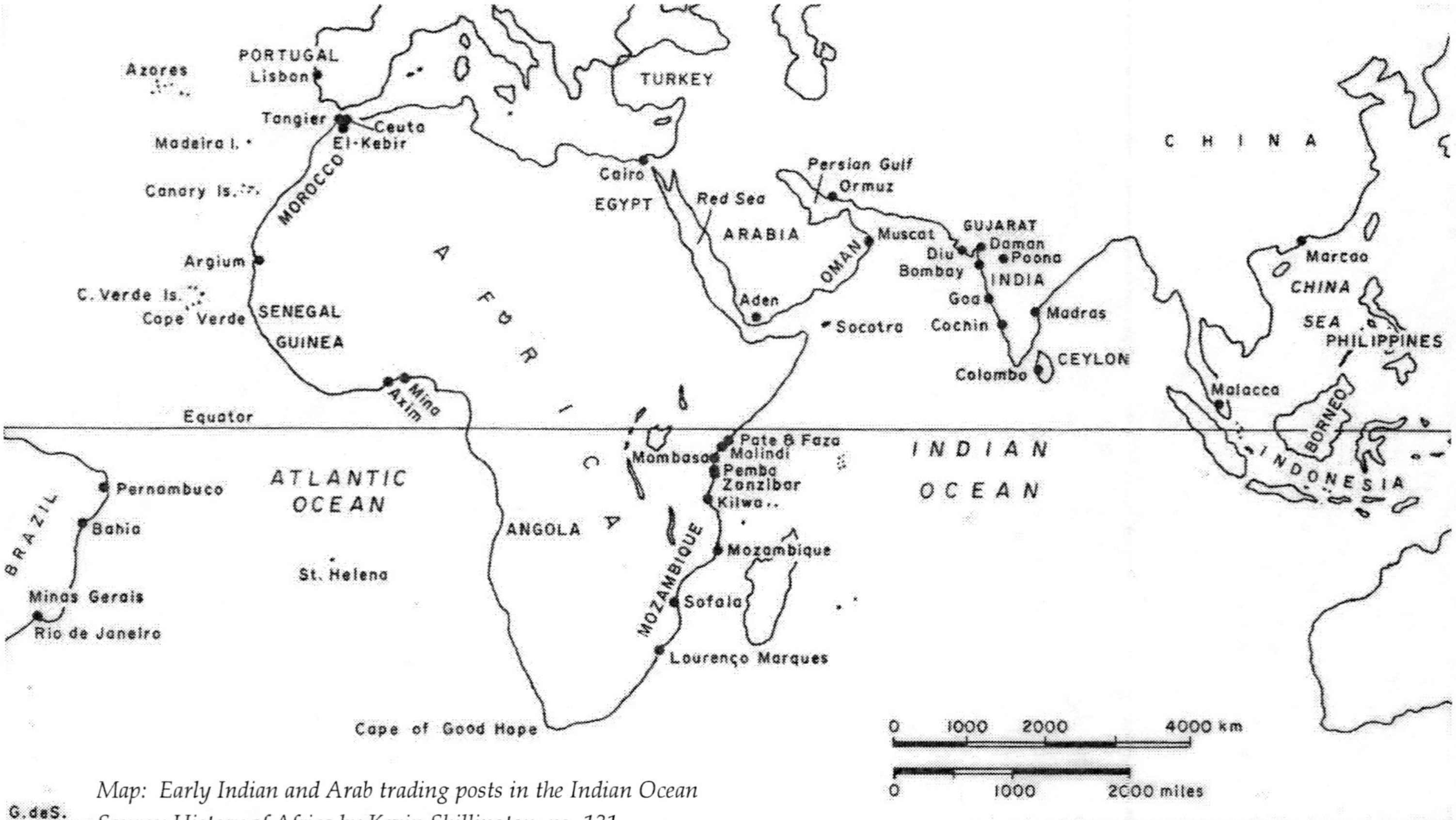

Map: Early Indian and Arab trading posts in the Indian Ocean
Source: History of Africa by Kevin Shillington, pg. 131.

Chapter 3

Indians in Africa

Indians are believed to have commenced their trading activities with southern Europe and northern Africa after settling on the coast of Syria where they had travelled overland. The existence of trade in *Vedic* times (1,500 BC - 500 BC) with distant countries has been undeniably established (Vaghella). In one of the four *Vedas,* the *Rig-Veda,* Indians are referred to as *Panis.* These people whom the Europeans described as 'non-Negroid and of Caucasian type' entered the continent of Africa from its northeast corner. The leader of these people was called *Yama,* the Lord of settlers, assembler of people, pathfinder. Yama seems to have come from the Indus Valley through Yemen, Egypt, Abyssinia (Ethiopia) and lastly following the course of the White Nile, to a land which the *Mahabarata* describes as 'Golden and sunny, very fertile and prosperous' roughly identified as Uganda. In the *Ramayana* the Red Sea is called 'Lohita Sagar' (East Africa Today, 1958-1959).

One major effect of the Azanian commerce with southern Arabia and India on the culture-history of Africa appears to be the introduction of iron working in East Africa. The first known iron-mongers in sub-Saharan Africa lived to the west of Lake Victoria. The first smelting may have started about 1,000 BC. The furnaces were small but elaborate; the hand worked bellows had carved wooden handles. It is believed that the technology came from India (Murdock, 1957). G.S. Were, in *East Africa Through a Thousand Years* mentions the existence of iron working west of Lake Victoria in pre-historic times. In this particular part of the country was also found the hump backed zebu an Asiatic breed of cattle with long horns, which may also have travelled to Africa along with these same Indians. This was probably the first contact of Indians with inland Africa.

In 1593 the Portuguese decided to build a fort at Mombasa strong enough to dominate the East African coast. It was to be called 'Jesus of Mombasa'. According to a letter dated 28, December 1611 the cost was to be met by the textile revenue from the port of Diu on the west coast of India and the 6% custom duty paid by all ships that called at the port of Mombasa. Eventually the cost was met by the port of Goa as Diu was unable to pay. About 30,000 to 40,000 stone masons, dressers and labourers came with the Monsoons from the Portuguese colonies of Damon, Diu and Goa (Strandes, 1961). Almost twenty years later the fort was not completed and by 1631 work had stopped completely as money and enthusiasm ran out. The Indian workmen found more lucrative occupations in the fast growing town of Mombasa.

Mauritius was uninhabited only four or five centuries ago, but from time immemorial India had established contact with her west side neighbour, Africa. Indo-Mauritian contact is said to have been made at least four centuries before European discovery of the islands. These islands were uninhabited and without a lot of capital outlay development was impossible by individuals. On their way to East Africa Indian sailors and traders touched the islands for fresh water and food. The proof was the Indian crow that had already established itself in the Mauritian jungle. It was an ingenious practice of the early Indian travellers to carry with them trained birds with strong wings on voyages to guide them to shore in case of stormy weather or other difficulties. This instinct of birds especially crows, to fly towards land was well known. There are references to shore-finding crows in the *Digha Nikaya* and the *Baveru Jataka* as having carried sailors to safety on their trading expeditions. This has been confirmed by the Dutch who were the first to actually live in Mauritius. The Indian crow in Mombasa most probably has the same origin.

Although the Portuguese had already 'acquired' Mauritius for themselves, they never lived there. The Dutch captured Mauritius from the Portuguese in 1638 and named it after Prince Maurice of Nassau. Later the French renamed it Ile de France. In 1810 after the Napoleonic wars, the British took possession of it and called it Mauritius.

Mauritius was largely a colony of slaves until 1835. Immigration of Indians from Bihar to Mauritius started in 1832. This was the earlier batch of indentured labour imported even before slavery was abolished under the French government, for the sugar plantations. After the abolition of slavery thousands of Indian indentured labourers were legally imported into Mauritius with the collaboration of the British Indian Government to work on the sugar plantations.

The other important industry in Mauritius, the silk industry, came into being on Indian convict labour. Convicts banished for life by the British colonialists were used in road building and other development projects. Charles Darwin who was in Mauritius in 1836 notes:

> Convicts from India are banished for life, at present there are 800 of them employed in various public works. Before seeing these people I had no idea that the inhabitants of India were such noble figures. These men are generally well conducted from their outward appearance, their cleanliness and their faithful observance of their strange religious rites.

According to Sir Bartle Frere the Indians had 'silently monopolized' a vast trade in East Africa between 1820 and 1870. During his journey from Mozambique to Cape Guardafui in 1873, Frere hardly met a shopkeeper who was not Indian. These included not only the *dukawallas* but also entrepreneurs and merchants.

> Indians are established in considerable numbers at all towns and villages on the opposite coast of the mainland also at Mozambique. The Khojas and Bohoras have settlements on the west coast of Madagascar and at French colonies of Nossi Beh and Myotte. The Hindus never bring their families but the Khojas and Bohoras bring their wives and families and become permanent settlers. In Madagascar and elsewhere along the coast the Indian owner assured me that though their oldest house was not more than sixty years standing their 'caste' had traded on the coast for ages past. (Rigby, 1861).

Early Indian presence in the Zimbabwe area is demonstrated by their making glass beads in Ingombe Ilembe, a craft they taught the Africans. The inland empire of Central Africa was called Monomotopa, named after

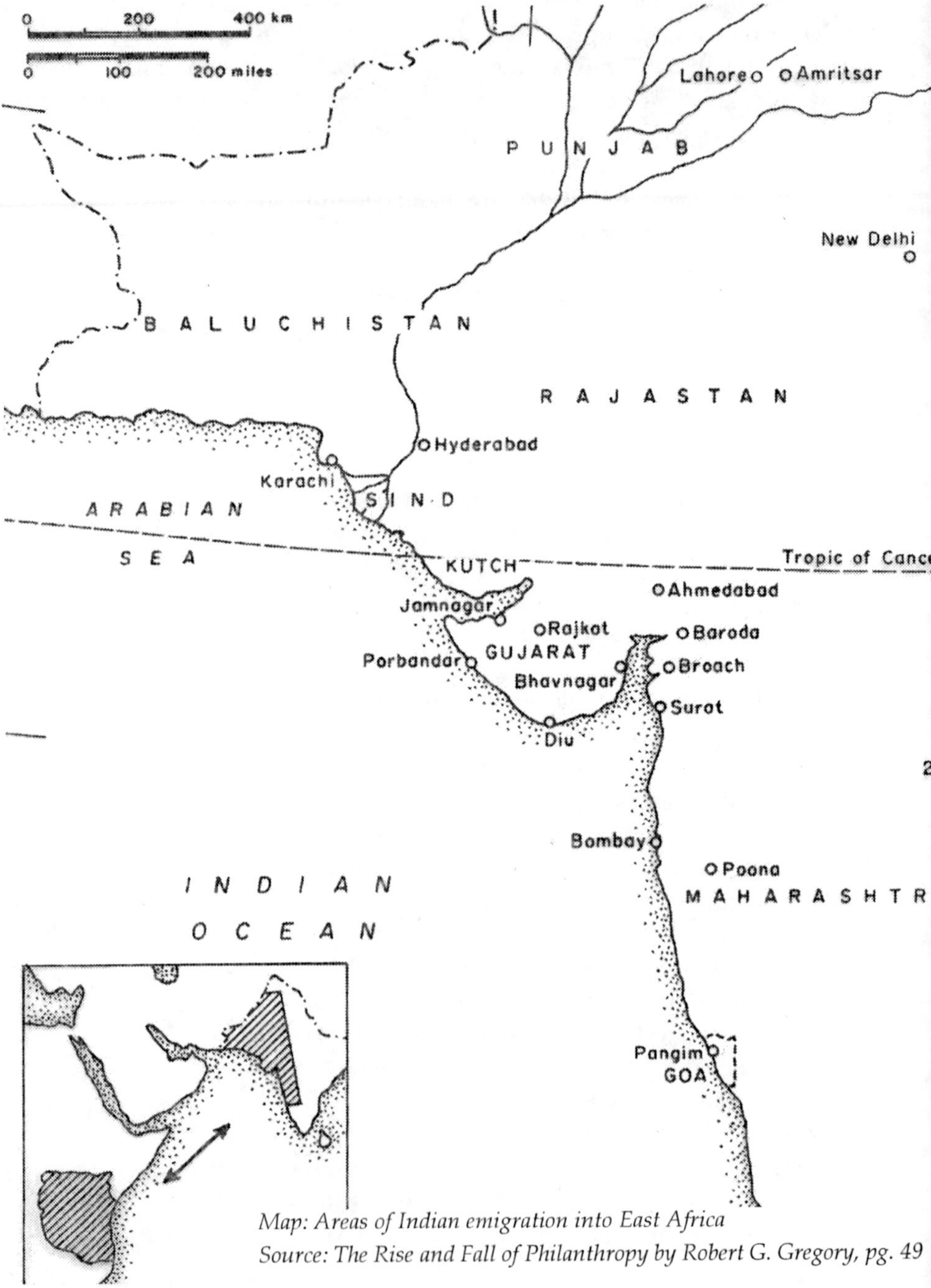

Map: Areas of Indian emigration into East Africa
Source: The Rise and Fall of Philanthropy by Robert G. Gregory, pg. 49

the King. This kingdom included Zimbabwe meaning 'Stone House', and Mozambique. On the basis of archeological evidence trade links between India and the eastern region of the Zambezi were always maintained. Even during the time of Arab and Portuguese piracy in the 15th century, cloth, glass, porcelain and Indian hemp reached this part of Africa in exchange for gold, copper and ivory.

The presence of Indians in Central Africa can be accounted for by the fact that Sir Harry Johnston was sent to found a colonial administration in Nyasaland (Malawi) with £10,000 a year. Johnston could only afford an armed force of seventy-five Indian soldiers with one British officer. Once again Britain had used her British Indian subjects to colonize and expand her empire in Africa.

Portuguese Goa was a beneficial source of immigration to Africa, a tropical paradise in every way except employment opportunity. The Portuguese colonists dominated the higher positions in the administration in Goa and there were too many educated Goans for the remaining jobs. Besides being poor administrators the Portuguese gave scant attention to development and the social structure of serfdom remained in place (Gregory, 1993). The Goans were forced to seek employment in British India and Portugal's other colonies in Africa.

Portugal failed to populate Angola and Mozambique with her own people but was successful in persuading Indians to settle in Mozambique. These traders and colonists from the East outnumbered the Portuguese and their number was such that Mousinho d'Albuquerque considered their presence a danger and urged restrictive measures.

There were two types of Indians in Mozambique. The first were the Banyans or Hindu traders from Indo-British houses of trade, who secured goods from the East India Company to exchange for products of Portuguese East Africa. These merchants were living along the coast, they did not settle in the colony nor did they invest in it and after a while they returned to India. The Portuguese generally regarded them with disfavour. The second type was the Goans or Canarins who had converted to Catholicism and who considered themselves Portuguese subjects. They made their home in Mozambique often marrying African women.

In 1661 Catherine of Bragança a Portuguese princess, married Charles II of Britain. England received Tangiers and Bombay as part of Catherine's dowry. This change brought many Portuguese Indians to Portuguese East Africa where they established a foothold in trade.

Both Goans and Indians involved in the administrative and clerical departments of the government did more good than harm to the colony. For two centuries the Indian kept alive small-scale trade in the interior. Writing in 1838, Torres Terugo describes the Indian as being the only industrious and respectable element in Mozambique society.

In Natal Province settlers mainly from Britain struggled to find a profitable basis of economic exploitation. In the 1850s it became apparent that there was a future for sugar plantations along the coast, but they lacked cheap and efficient labour. Africans were unused to wage labour under plantation conditions. The South Africans then turned to indentured labour from India. In the 1860s the first batch of Indian labourers began to arrive in Natal. Of the 143,000 Indians that came to South Africa only 27,000 returned home. By 1936 the number of Indians was 219,928 of whom at least half were born in South Africa.

The source of all immigration after 1890 was northwest India, Punjab, where most indentured labour emanated from. Although fertile and well watered it was over populated. Sindh another area of recruitment is a desert, where it was difficult to make a living. Gujerat, Kathiawar and Cutch although generally fertile were prone to drought and famine. (Gregory, 1993).

For the Ithnasheries and Ismailis religion was a motivation to emigrate to Islamic states where they received better treatment. There were many opportunities in business, consequently the Shahs, Patels, and Ismailis abandoned their traditional farming to engage in business. (Gregory, 1993). The other reason for preferring trade could have been that although the Patels were a farming community the British land policy of white farmers, forced them to change their traditional profession to business. (Samson, 1993)

The Parsees, a small group of immigrants to India from Persia who settled in the Bombay area became highly successful traders and bankers. Industry, ingenuity, thrift and education brought wealth to these people who had left their motherland to seek their fortunes. Originally from Persia (Iran) followers of Prophet Zoroaster, they suffered persecution at the hands of the Muslims and had to flee for safety to Hormuz in 740 AD. But the refuge was shortlived and they set out for India. The first group settled on a small island called Diu and finally in Bombay. The exact date of their settlement in Bombay is not known, but it is from there that a section of the community settled in Zanzibar some time before 1668. A small group of Parsees also found its way to south central Africa, perhaps from Hormuz. It was also thought that the stone tower of Greater Zimbabwe was built by them, but it has been established that the ruins were the work of Africans three centuries earlier.

In many parts of Africa there were three communities, African, European and Indian, ranged in accordance with a descending order of pigmentation in all aspects of their lives, whether privilege, opportunity, education or standard of living. The Indians were the most under privileged of the minority groups. They suffered the disabilities of the underprivileged without the compensation of inner security and long-range certainties that enabled the African majority to face the future with confidence. This uncertainty, arising from the conviction that there was no security on the continent dominated their thinking.

> The threat of being ground between the upper and nether stones of the multiracial mill was too great to permit any relaxation of vigilance. (Herskovits, 1958).

Indians in Africa at that time were not concerned with the production of goods except on a subsistence level. They were not interested in land or exploration or colonization. Being purely traders their interest was entirely economic, they merely financed the collection and were responsible for the distribution and sale of goods. These traders had settled all along the East African coast. They were in possession of the best trade from Aden to Sofala and across the Mozambican Channel on the west coast of Madagascar, including the Comoros Isles.

Indians in East Africa

East Africa: Land of Pukka Sahibs.

(George Padmore In *Britain's Third Empire, MCMXLIX*)

Indians for thousands of years were at the heart of the economic activity which brought the outside world to the East African coast. Indian commercial relations with the East African coast started centuries before the building of the Uganda railway. There can be no doubt that traders from Arabia, Persia and India had been visiting the East African coast since before 1,000 BC. By AD 1,000 there were established markets and settlements on the coast. In 1497, when the Portuguese rounded the Cape of Good Hope they found Indian traders at every port along the East African coast and a very considerable trade carried on between India and Africa.

The *Periplus* mentions an important and extensive trade between Ariake (modern Konkan) and Barugaza (modern Broach). Vasco da Gama found Indians especially 'Calicut men' in Mozambique, Kilwa, Mombasa and Malindi.

> They came to Sofala in small boats *zambucos* from the kingdoms of Kilwa, Mombasa and Melinde bringing cloth, white and blue. Also silk and many small beads grey, red, yellow. Which things come to those kingdoms from the great Kingdom of Cambay in greater ships. Carrying from Aden, cotton, drugs and gems, seed pearls, carnelians, opium, copper, quick silver, vermilion, rose water, woolen cloth, coloured Mecca carpets, gold coins, rice, sugar, coconuts, sandalwood, musk, so much so that this place has a greater and richer trade than any in the world. (Duarte Barbosa).

Indians in East Africa took to trade and commerce as the main economic pursuit of their lives from the early days of their settlement. Their commercial activities were initially confined to the coastal belt of Kenya and Tanganyika and to the Zanzibar markets and later to Uganda in the wake of the building of the Uganda Railway.

However the Indian population in the East African region even before the construction of the railway, already included a substantial group of merchants numbering about 7,000 based in Zanzibar and in the main coastal towns. But in spite of the very early association with the coast, Indian settlement consisted of a minority element. From 1895-96 Indians were confined mainly to the East African coast. Capt. Thomas Boteler in his *Narrative of a Voyage of Discovery to Africa and Arabia 1821-1826 . . . under the Command of Captain F. W. Owens . . .* observed:

> There are a few instances of Indian traders like Allidina Visram, Adamjee Alibhoy and M.G. Puri who penetrated into the East African interior even before Sir George Whitehouse stepped ashore in Mombasa in 1895 to conduct the building of the railway. (Boteler, 1935)

Indians played a significant role in the development of the East African countries. They were sailors, merchants, financiers and administrators. As the volume of trade increased by the early 19th century, a growing number of Indian merchants established themselves in Zanzibar, Kilwa, Bagamoyo, Pangani, Tanga, Malindi and Mombasa. They did little wholesale business at the various posts except for importation of goods to supply to the caravans going inland for bartering local produce. Rarely did they penetrate the hinterland. As Sir Bartle Frere said:

> The *banyans* usually keep to the ports, they are content to sit at the coast and wax rich as commercial bankers.

However there was one Nanji Musa an Ismaili, who came to be known as Musa Mzuri, a pioneer trader in the Kaze (Tabora) area in the 1830s. Musa welcomed Speke and from him Speke learnt much about Lake Victoria and the Mountains of the Moon, information that was helpful to him in his exploration. And as Arab power declined more and more of the trade of the coast fell into Indian hands.

Indian merchants' influence extended 6,000 miles along the East African coast. The Indian trader became the most influential and permanent element of the trading community. By working their way inland from the coast, their influence extended into several other business undertakings as well, first through their trading talents and later by supplying the much needed artisan skills and subordinate services which the white settlers found uneconomical to provide. Through hard work and without any assistance from the British Government, they achieved success and distinction as skilled craftsmen, doctors, dentists, lawyers, plantation managers, bankers, businessmen and government officials.
Sir Bartle Frere remarked:

> Hardly a loan can be negotiated, a mortgage effected or a bill cashed, import or export of cargo without Indian agency.

Indian enterprise made a substantial contribution to the economic development of East Africa by boosting the collection of taxes and obtaining sufficient money to free the colony of its debt to the Imperial British Government in loans for the building of the Uganda Railway. However there were also other concerns for the Colonial Government. In 1899 Sir Harry Johnston wrote:

> The building of the railway means 15,000 coolies hundreds of clerks, draughtsmen, mechanics, surveyors and policemen. The Indian postal system, Indian coinage . . .

As pointed out earlier there already was a significant number of Indians living in East Africa even before the railway construction began. These Indians with their numbers now increased took advantage of the commercial opportunities and administrative posts, pioneering the local trading centers and Indian bazaars in the districts. They introduced the local population to imported goods and the Indian rupee, as well as overseeing the transition from a barter-based economy to a money-based economy. The Indians were from the earliest days what they still are in East Africa today, masters of finance, bankers, money-changers and money-lenders.
H.S. Newman says in Banyani:

> None work harder and for longer hours rendering to our trade in East Africa. Their industry is a tropical marvel . . .

Besides the traders and enterprising fortune seekers, Indians were also brought to East Africa on various assignments. When Seyyid Said moved his capital from Muscat to Zanzibar in 1840 his bodyguard was made up of men from Baluchistan. In 1895 a special contingent of 300 Indian troops was recruited for the Uganda Railway. In 1896 Indians were brought in to build the railway since Africans would not undertake such labour at that time. In 1897 a contingent of 300 Indian troops similar to that in 1895, was recruited to put down a mutiny by Sudanese troops. In 1913 the King's African Rifles (K.A.R.) received another contingent of 300 troops from India.

After the 'scramble for Africa' many Indians crossed over from Equatorial Africa to East Africa. The newcomers found that the colonial structure offered increased opportunities for commercial skills based on industry, enterprise and thrift.

Indians have been an indispensable force in creating commerce and wealth in all East African territories with their productive activities. The *dukawallah* and *fundi* carried his skills to remote parts of the country. The Goan community was invaluable in both administrative and culinary capacities.

The importance of India in the Indian Ocean is due not only to its geographical location but also to historical factors. As controllers of the Indian Ocean trade India became the foundation for empires built by European powers.

> But for the Indians we should not be there now [East Africa]. It was entirely through gaining possession of these Indian merchants that we were enabled to build up influence that eventually resulted in our position.
> (Sir John Kirk giving evidence to the Sanderson Committee, 1910.)

Chapter 4

The Sultanate of Zanzibar

Although the Indian Ocean trade was centuries old, neither Arabs nor Indians were interested in settlement in East Africa. However disputes over the succession of Prophet Muhammad divided the Arab Empire causing some of the losing side especially from Oman, to take refuge on the pleasant coast of East Africa with which they were already familiar through trade. At that time in the case of the Omanis, trade was not the only inducement to found settlements, relief from internal strife brought about by changes of government, was an added incentive. In the 7th century AD the Arabian tribes brought together the Asiatic peoples of Persia (Iran), Irak (Iraq) and Oman who had settled on the East African coast, by converting them to Islam. Mombasa and Malindi became important centers of Arab power.

The first Arabs to settle on the East African coast were known as Ithnashara Twaifa or Twelve Tribes; Thalatha Twaifa (three tribes) and Tisa Twaifa (nine tribes). In Mombasa these early settlers were simply known as the 'Twelve Tribes'. *(The South and East Africa Yearbook & Guide, 1948)*. There is no definite information about the exact date of settlement. In AD 975 they were joined by Hassan bin Ali and his six sons from Persia who arrived in a fleet of seven ships. The whole of the East African coast was under the influence of the Twelve Tribes, as they called themselves.

The chief ports of settlement north to south were, Mogadishu, Barava, Siu, Pate, Lamu, Malindi, Kilifi, Mombasa, Vumba, Pemba, Zanzibar, Mafia, Kilwa, Comoros Isles and Mozambique. Among the coastal settlements the State of Kilwa was the leading settlement. The *Kilwa Chronicle* tells how Hassan bin Ali bought the island from the African Chief whose price was as much coloured cloth as stretched round the entire island, which was about fifteen miles. At this time Kilwa was an island only at high tide. In 1498 Vasco da Gama found that Kilwa not

Zanzibar, was the most important center of trade.

When the Portuguese reached Mombasa, then called 'Mvita' (island of war) the whole coast was known as the Zenj (black) Empire. The East African coast has been part of the large Indian Ocean trade complex throughout the Christian era. Trading centers along the Red Sea and on the islands and mainland between Somalia and Mozambique have a long complex history. The *Periplus* describes a significant trade between Rome and India. In this trade some of the port cities of the Red Sea became collecting points for the exchange of goods of the Eastern African area. The author says that the trade was regulated and controlled by a ruler located in Southern Arabia. Portuguese piracy and looting greatly reduced trade, however in the 1700s trading resumed in the old manner carried on by the Persians, Omanis and Indians.

The most important town on the East African coast was Rhapta; Mombasa seems to have been relatively insignificant at this time. Zanzibar which only appears on European maps in the 12th century had long been a center of trade even as to include China within its radius (Gordon-Brown, 1957). According to Arab geographers, Zanghistan, from which Zanzibar or the Zanj (negro or black) coast is derived, covered the whole of the eastern part of Africa. Zanj is equivalent to the Sanskrit word 'Sankh' probably from the *Puranas,* Sankh-Dwipa meaning 'Island of Shells'. (Kotecha, 1994)

Some time after the expulsion of the Portuguese from Mombasa in about 1593 the Omani ruler sent Governors and garrisons from Muscat to the most important towns on the East African coast. One of the Governors was of the Mazrui clan. By the 18th century the East African coastal cities began to fight each other with the encouragement given by the Omani Governors to the Arab settlers from Muscat, who had been trading in East Africa long before Seyyid Said came to claim his possessions there. These Governors proved to be no better than the Portuguese. There was civil war in Pate, Malindi, Pemba, Mafia and Kilwa. They were at war with Oman and with each other. Only Mombasa managed to sustain its independence under the leadership of the Mazrui family from the time the first Mazrui became Deputy Governor in 1727 until the advent of Seyyid Said in 1873. The third Governor appointed by the Omani Imam to Mombasa, Muhammed ibn Uthman al-Mazrui, was executed in 1741 by the new Omani Imam, Ahmed ibn Said al-Busaidi, Seyyid Said's father. However Muhammed's son Ali ibn Uthman al-Mazrui, later regained control of

Mombasa.

The 'King of Zinjibar, Salim bin Ahmed al-Mazrui lives in Mamsa'. Since 1746 the Mazrui clan had held Fort Jesus, they also laid claim to Pemba the fertile island, for their food needs. The Mazruis sought British protection for Mombasa against Seyyid Said in order to take complete control of Mombasa.

Capt. F.W. Owen, Commander of the Leven of the Royal Navy who had travelled to Bombay (1821-1826), was now on his way back to East Africa. When he heard about the Mazruis' 'offer' of Mombasa to the British in exchange for protection, he thought it was a 'heaven-sent chance to establish British presence on the East African coast to stifle the slave trade'. Capt. Owen was convinced of Britain's greater role in this part of Africa. He wrote to the Admiralty:

> It is clear to me as the sun that God has prepared the dominion of East Africa for the only nation on earth that has public virtue enough to govern it for its own benefit, and the only nation on earth that takes the revealed word as their moral law. (Hall, 1996).

Owen urged Britain to buy from Seyyid Said all the East African possessions paying him in perpetuity as much as he was paid from the collection in revenue. He drew up his terms for bestowing British protection on Mombasa guaranteeing the Mazruis rule over the Sultan's 'former' possessions and promising a British Agent resident in Fort Jesus. Owen appointed John Reitz first Governor of Mombasa. He soon realized that the Mazruis only wanted the Union Jack above Fort Jesus to scare Seyyid Said and that they had no intention of becoming British subjects. Unfortunately for Owen also, Reitz died of malaria four months after he was appointed Governor and the Mazruis were left to deal with their problem with Seyyid Said alone.

In 1784 Ahmad ibn Said al Busaidi died in Muscat, capital of Oman, and in 1806 Seyyid Said bin Sultan became the sole ruler of Oman at the age of sixteen. The Omani Arabs had a long history of shipping, trading and settling on the East African coast, but by the 19th century when they came in larger numbers the influx was encouraged by Imam Seyyid Said from Oman. Omani dynasties had held important possessions on the East

African coast since the 17th century. That the Imams of Oman were unable to consolidate their position in Africa earlier, was largely due to their own weakness at home. After 1820 when Seyyid Said's efforts to enlarge his Persian Empire failed he turned his attention to his East African possessions. His first visit to Zanzibar was in 1828. His visits became more frequent until in 1840 he established his capital there.

Sultan Seyyid Said (1806-1856)

'I am nothing but a merchant.'

Seyyid Said ascended the throne of Oman and Zanzibar in 1806. Seyyid Said, called the Merchant Prince, recognized the importance of trade as an economic factor in the enrichment of himself and his realm. In 1840 he made Zanzibar his principal residence.

Indian traders from Cutch, Porbandar and Surat had been traditionally active in the Persian Gulf and in Muscat in particular, for centuries. Helped by their special aptitude for business they won the confidence of the Imams as financiers and customs collectors. While in Oman, Seyyid Said had done his best to attract those indispensable banyans of whom there were already about a thousand residing in Muscat.

> Nor had ever a Government more useful, more steady-working and inoffensive protegés. Interferring with no one, seeking nothing beyond their direct line of business. Unobtrusive, courteous and above all skilled in the mysteries of the ledger and the counter.

Previously Seyyid Said had used all his powers to lure these Indians to Muscat from India, now he was offering them the same incentives to move with him to Zanzibar.

Seyyid Said, the youthful Imam of Oman, was intent on restoring Arab hegemony over Zanzibar and the string of Swahili settlements on the mainland. He made his first visit to Zanzibar in 1828 and decided it would suit him better than Oman, but he was anxious to keep the plan from the British, the self-proclaimed overlords and guardians of the peace in the

Indian Ocean. Indians were numerous in Muscat as part of their network of trade and finance. In Zanzibar Seyyid Said turned to them for accounting and banking, but the one business he kept tightly in Arab hands was the slave trade.

It was trade above all else that drew Seyyid Said to Zanzibar but he also had as his aims power, prestige and security, and to attain them, wealth was needed and that could only come through trade. The pattern of Seyyid Said's policy in Zanzibar was based on the existing framework in Muscat. He encouraged the Indians who had been working in Muscat for at least a century and in particular those whom he had been working with, to join him in Zanzibar purely as financial advisers. In 1832, on one of his visits to Zanzibar, he brought with him Bhatia merchants from Muscat.

Seyyid Said, the first resident Sultan of Zanzibar, fostered the growth of the Indian community in Zanzibar by giving them complete religious, social and economic freedom and by personal relationships with the ablest of men, using them for administrative and financial services. Banking, finance and commerce were in Indian hands along with the wholesale and retail trade. Hindus and Arabs were natural enemies, but through diplomacy, Seyyid Said cemented an alliance between the enterprising Indians and the warlike Arabs. Seyyid Said understood well the value of trade as a source of wealth, he also knew that his own Omani Arabs were of little use for trade and would never attain real success without the cooperation and leadership of the Indian merchants.

In 1840 when Seyyid Said made Zanzibar his principle residence, a class of Arab plantation owners became his court, living a life of idleness and luxury. Others arrived from Muscat to exploit the mainland markets, borrowing money from Indian usurers and disappearing up-country for years. They bought slaves who worked on their plantations while they travelled. Seyyid Said knew that the commercial transactions of his own people however well intentioned, would never attain real importance in trade. Seyyid Said knew Zanzibar's economic importance emanated from its trade goods coming from the African interior, so he directed his energies to the exploitation of the interior. He encouraged the immigration of Indians partly as a means of marketing the clove and coconut products and partly as an agency for financing the caravans to the interior of the African mainland.

In the palace garden at Mtoni in Zanzibar the first clove plantation was started in 1828 with seedlings from Mauritius. The clove was introduced into Mauritius and Bourbon (Réunion) from Moluccus, Indonesia and later into Zanzibar. Pearce in *Zanzibar* ascribes the introduction of cloves to a Crèole from Ile de France (Bourbon) about 1800 (Coupland, 1938).

When Seyyid Said, an exceptional ruler, moved his capital from Muscat, Oman, to Zanzibar in 1840 he found the Indians already well established in trade. He exploited the fertility of the soil by arbitrarily compelling the Arab planters under threat of confiscation of their land, to plant cloves to the exclusion of all other crops. He resisted the general opinion which was contrary to his decision, for in 1872 Burton insisted that sugarcane, not cloves should be the main crop of Zanzibar. By 1844 Zanzibar and Pemba produced 80% of the world's cloves, and the whole crop was handled by Indian merchants.

The development of Zanzibar from a village into the most important trading center along the East African coast was due to the organizational skills of Seyyid Said. His economic policies included advancement of the Indian community to finance economic growth and to consolidate clove-growing in Zanzibar and Pemba, already begun before his arrival. The key to Seyyid Said's success in Zanzibar was coordination and expansion of available resources. The trade routes were already established, now the size and number of caravans going into the African interior were greatly increased. The trading centers in Tabora and Ujiji on Lake Tanganyika were developed and contact was also made with the Baganda of Uganda in 1844.

In 1893 Seyyid Said revolutionized the monetary system by replacing the European silver Maria Therèsa dollar and Spanish crown with the copper coinage of India. The Sultan also simplified the customs collection. He maintained constant communication with England, New York, Peking and India through his ships which were repaired in Bombay. Under Seyyid Said, Zanzibar became an Indian emporium which was quickly followed by German, French, American and British houses of trade. Sultan Seyyid Said concluded commercial treaties with America 1833, Britain 1839, France 1844. Under Seyyid Said Zanzibar became a port of call for the ships of the world.

Sultan Seyyid Said well understood the relationship between commerce and capital, hence he was at pains to encourage immigration of Indian bankers who were granted control of the financial administration in Zanzibar, including the all-important Customs collection. Jairam Sewji the Customs Master gave Seyyid Said $310,000 per year for his private expenses; in spite of that he was always in debt. In Seyyid Said's day and probably for many generations before, nearly all the business of Arab banking, the financing and commercial enterprise, the wholesale and most of the retail trade on which the prosperity of East Africa depended, was in Indian hands.

Meanwhile trade flourished and wherever the Sultan's red flag was hoisted, Indians who had been trading on that coast from earliest times until driven away by the Portuguese, would flock back. It was the establishment of the 'Muscat Arab' which contributed to the rise of Zanzibar becoming the chief market in the world for ivory, gum copal, and cloves. As Rigby remarked, 'The trade of this port with India is becoming very important.'

To absorb the products of East Africa Seyyid Said had to find new markets beyond the Middle and Far East. He warmly welcomed the first incursions of Western trade avoided since the days of Portuguese empire-building. He encouraged merchants from the western world to trade with his dominions. He did not realize at the time that he was jeopardizing his throne, for on the west coast of Africa trade mainly in slaves, had been followed by colonization. Besides, western trade together with missionary and humanitarian aid marked the end of any hope the Africans might have had of developing their own culture and government.

Seyyid Said took a fancy to an American trader, Edmund Roberts, to whom he complained about the British. However, despite the show of friendship towards the Americans, they were charged the same duty as the British in the Indian Ocean possessions of the Sultan. Earlier, Roberts had struck up a friendship with the Customs Master Jairam Sewji, a friendship frowned upon by the British.

Roberts advised the American Government to establish diplomatic relations with the Zanzibar Government for purposes of trade. His Government responded in 1832 when President Jackson appointed Roberts as a Special Agent to negotiate the treaty. On 21, September 1833 the first agreement between Seyyid Said and a foreign government was signed in Muscat. In this Treaty of Commerce the most profitable section of the East African coast called Mrima, situated between Pangani and Kilwa, producing ivory and gum copal, was offered to American trade as a monopoly. The only people who ignored the monopoly were the

Indians, who just hoisted the Sultan's red flag and proceeded with their trading.

In 1839 Seyyid Said signed a Treaty of Commerce with the British Government. Soon after that he appealed to the British Government to appoint a 'genuine wise Englishman . . . all true pure English and not of other nations'. He was hoping for an Englishman from Britain, being disenchanted with the high-handed stiff upper-lip ways of officials from British India. But to his disappointment Prime Minister Palmeston appointed an Irishman, Atkins Hamerton from India, because he knew Hindustani. Seyyid Said concluded a Treaty of Commerce with France in 1844.

Seyyid Said's death in 1856 deprived the Indians of his clarity of purpose especially needed now that forces from Europe began to influence decisions of the succeeding Sultans. The British had exerted pressure in Zanzibar through a Permanent Resident, but Seyyid Said's diplomatic skills had minimized this influence even to the extent of maintaining the Slave Trade despite a Treaty of 1845 to end the traffic between Zanzibar and Muscat. He described his fall from 'golden years' to the 'less favourable treatment given to the *banyans* by the British'.

Following the death of Sultan Seyyid Said a dispute arose on the succession in Zanzibar as well as in Oman. The controversy was settled through the mediation of Lord Canning, Governor General of India. It was called the 'Canning Award' of April 1861, whereby the Sultanate of Zanzibar was separated from the Imamate of Oman. Since Oman had nothing to offer the world but dates and dried fish, Zanzibar was ordered to pay Muscat 40,000 Maria Therèsa dollars a year. This was no hardship, for Zanzibar's revenue collection was considerable.

Seyyid Said's Successors

Seyyid Said had several sons but only four are worth mentioning as his successors and of these, Sultan Seyyid Bargash is the only one who made some significant impact on Zanzibar's history. Also, since they had different mothers, there was not much love among them which resulted in a great deal of intrigue. The British exerted considerable influence on the succession, carefully choosing the one who would best promote Britain's interests.

Thuwain, Seyyid Said's eldest son was appointed regent in Oman when his father moved his capital to Zanzibar. Thuwain ruled in Muscat and possessed a navy, but if he wished to lay claim to his father's throne in Zanzibar he had to travel 2,000 miles with his navy, before he could do so. Thuwain and Bargash were both jealous of Majid, a younger brother, because they knew that he had the support of the British in his claim to the Zanzibar throne. Thuwain's efforts to put together an invasion force were quickly stopped by the British who intercepted his fleet, forcing him to return to Muscat.

So now, Thuwain was kept in Oman and Seyyid Bargash, a strong contender for the Zanzibar throne was exiled in Bombay. He was provided with a large house, carriage and a generous allowance. Abd al-Aziz, another younger brother seen as a potential trouble maker, was also packed off to India to prevent interference in Britain's plans for Zanzibar.

Sultan Seyyid Majid (1856-1870)

In 1856 Seyyid Majid succeeded his father Sultan Seyyid Said, to the throne of Zanzibar. He enjoyed the support of the British who wanted a weak, sickly ruler in Zanzibar, nevertheless he still evaded any stoppage of the slave trade contrary to what the British had expected. Rigby who had hoped to manipulate him, had supported his claim against his brothers'. Seyyid Majid's revenue was large, 206,000 crowns (about 443,000 rupees) a year, but his treasury was always empty because of his extravagance. He owed Ladha Damji the Collector of Customs at the time, 327 crowns and was always in debt. So even the Sultan had to borrow from the Indians.

For many years Ladha Damji was the most influential person under the Sultans. He was not only the Customs Master but also the confidante of the Sultan. Burton said of him,

> With the exception of Ladha on whom he is entirely dependent for money, Majid had not a single honest person about him on whose oath he can rely.

Burton thought the Royal Treasury was managed with extreme simplicity.

> When the Prince wants goods or cash he writes an order upon his Collector of Customs. The draft is kept as an authority to be produced every three to four years upon general balancing.

Colonel Rigby who was a committed abolitionist was frustrated with Majid's resistance to abolishing the slave trade. On the other hand Majid was also unpopular with his own people because of the influence the British were exerting on him and they often attacked his palace. After three years Rigby was promoted to General and transferred. But that was not the end of Majid's problems. His health was failing and Seyyid Bargash who he thought had been banished for life, reappeared in Zanzibar after two years in Bombay. The British knew of Majid's failing health and Bargash had been brought back in readiness for his demise. Bargash was also aware of that so he was content to wait.

With everything that was going on around him Sultan Majid became so paranoid that he hid on the mainland. With his wealth he founded a new city called Dar es Salaam 'Harbour of Peace', a port on the mainland which he intended to make his new capital. Majid died in Dar es Salaam in 1870 and the way was clear for Seyyid Bargash to become Sultan of Zanzibar.

Sultan Seyyid Bargash (1870-1888)

On Sultan Majid's death Seyyid Bargash became Sultan of Zanzibar. Bargash who had been exiled in Bombay by the British at the time of his father Sultan Seyyid Said's death, blamed the Indians (Hindus) for Majid's ascension to the throne of Zanzibar, so out of revenge on the *banyans* he appointed an Ismaili merchant, Tharya Topan to the firm of Ladha Damji.

Two aspects of the Indian trader are exemplified by the policies of Seyyid Bargash. At first he tried to wriggle out of a debt he inherited from his predecessor to Jairam Sewji, demonstrating his anti-Indian feelings. Yet later in his reign he leaned heavily on a number of Indians for money and advice. He established cordial relations with Indian businessmen as evidenced by the barazas he held on the ground floor of his palace from 10.00 am to 11.00 am and from 8.00 pm to 9.00 pm. daily. The prominent men of all the Indian and African communities attended.

The richest businessmen in East Africa were in Zanzibar. It was during Seyyid Bargash's reign that Indians of all communities settled in Zanzibar in large numbers. The Sultan kept in touch with these businessmen through an informal legislative council, the *Barazas*. Events discussed were, world news and the European market with special reference to Zanzibar, at the end of which a consensus was taken.

Following are the names of those who attended:

Bohora - Pirbhai Jivanjee, Ebrahimjee Walijee
Ismaili - Pira Dewji, Tharya Topan, Nassur Lallani
Banyan - Ibji Sivji, Jairam Sewji, Damadar Jairam

Soon after Seyyid Bargash became Sultan of Zanzibar the Imperial Government took up the subject of slavery with him in response to the reports sent to England by Dr. Livingstone, on the evils of the Slave Trade. Sir Bartle Frere a senior member of the Indian Government was ordered to go to Zanzibar in January 1873 with a letter from Queen Victoria regarding the abolition of the slave trade in Bargash's dominions. Months went by and Bargash had done nothing about the letter. He argued that the clove trade would suffer with the shortage of labour. What Bargash did not know was that the Royal Navy was on its way to Zanzibar and that if the Treaty was not signed, Zanzibar would be blockaded.

During Seyyid Said's reign the British had exerted pressure on him to honour the Treaty of 1845 to end the slave traffic between Zanzibar and Muscat. Seyyid Bargash found himself under similar but more intense pressure and ultimately a treaty was forced on him by Sir John Kirk to end the trade.

Beside the Abolition Treaty there was the other irksome matter of a Concession to Sir William Mackinnon's Company of all Bargash's mainland ports from Dar es Salaam to Kilwa for seventy-five years for 'trade and evangelizing'. In this venture Mackinnon was encouraged by Sir John Kirk, a fellow Scotsman. This worried Bargash because he did not actually understand what all this meant to him, so once again he delayed signing the agreement. Fortuntely for Bargash the matter died down for lack of commitment on the part of Mackinnon's Company. Eventually he signed a new version of the Concession to the British Government allowing it to collect custom duty at Mombasa, paying the Sultan in perpetuity almost all the revenue collected and flying the Sultan's flag over Fort Jesus, in return for using the port.

The next aggravation in Seyyid Bargash's life, the Berlin Conference of 1884 which aimed to maintain free trade in tropical Africa, left Bargash without empire and without illusions (Hall, 1996). He had lost effective control of his realm. Bargash informed Tippu Tip a former slave turned ivory merchant:

> I must beg your forgiveness. I no longer have any hope of keeping the interior. The Europeans are after my possessions. Happy are those who died before now and know nothing of this. (Hall, 1996).

On 27 February 1885 Chancellor Bismark released a Proclamation signed by Kaiser Wilhelm declaring a Protectorate over parts of the African mainland facing Zanzibar. He based his claim on twelve 'treaties' which a young German, Carl Peters, had secretly brought home from an expedition to the small communities of Usegula, Ugura, Usagara, and Ukami, whereby about a 150 mile stretch of the coast was 'offered' by their Chiefs to the Society for German Colonization.

By now Seyyid Bargash was very ill, 'his political anxieties are wearing him fast' wrote Stanley in 1887. Bargash was then fifty-four, he clung to life for another year. He left behind two very young sons and only one wife. When his sons were infants Bargash had asked the British to look after them and guarantee their succession in the event of his death while they were still minors. Britain declined on the grounds that that would be 'construed as interference' under an Anglo-French Treaty on Zanzibar's independence.

Since the British had the port of Mombasa they were no longer interested in Zanzibar. The Germans were now behaving as if Zanzibar belonged to them. Trade was at its lowest ebb. Most of the rich Indian merchants had moved to British East Africa (later Kenya) with the building of the Uganda Railway and 'almost the last shreds of Zanzibar's independence were buried with Sultan Seyyid Bargash in March 1888.' (Hall, 1996).

Sultan Khalifa, 1888

On Sultan Seyyid Bargash's death his younger brother Khalifa, inherited the Zanzibar throne with the backing of the new colonial overlords, the Germans. Khalifa had been confined in an underground chamber by Sultan Bargash to prevent him from seizing power. This resulted in his becoming mentally unhinged.

Only a month after being installed as Sultan he granted the German East Africa Company a fifty-one year lease over the entire East African coastal region from Dar es Salaam to Bagamoyo, the Indian Ocean terminus to the main caravan routes from the interior of Africa. He had enough good sense left to insist that all tax-collection should be done under his flag. The Germans however had no intentions of keeping any agreements at all.

Trouble began when the Germans decided to raise their own flag in Bagamoyo. Since hundreds of dhows from Zanzibar were constantly arriving in Bagamoyo to land their trade goods and collect the exports from the interior, Arab emissaries protested that the German flag was a violation of the agreement. Further up the coast in Pangani there was destruction of property by the Germans and the Sultan's flag was pulled down and stamped upon. The Arabs were intimidated in their show of opposition by the presence of German warships lying off-shore and with the constant threat of bombardment.

The first resistance came on 4, September 1888 from Sheikh Abushiri bin Salim, a wealthy sugar plantation owner. In his view Sultan Khalifa had no right to hand over the coast to anyone. But the rebellion had no chance of success. The Germans with their modern weapons landed their forces in two groups, at Bagamoyo and Dar es Salaam. Britain took part in the sea blockade by preventing ammunition from reaching bin Salim. He was captured and beheaded.

Sultan Seyyid Hamoud bin Mahomed, 1891

There was no fanfare over Seyyid Hamoud bin Mahomed, one more of Seyyid Said's sons' ascension to the throne of Zanzibar. The Times of London carried an item on the new, 'acceptable' Sultan Seyyid Hamoud bin Mahomed who was 'in complete accord with his English advisers'. In 1893 he signed a Decree on the gradual suppression of the slave trade. By the twentieth century Zanzibar was only a memory of past glory.

How the Empire of the Sultans of Zanzibar was gradually broken up

Africa was the political chessboard on which European nations that possessed the courage and Empire lust that the Arabs once had, played their game. The rule of the Sultans was never very effective on mainland Tanganyika, so European nations one after another rushed in to snatch what they could in the latter half of the 19th century. England was the first. When she began grabbing, German land-lust and jealousy were aroused. Similarly, the Italians acquired the Somaliland coast north of Kisumayu. These three nations in particular enriched and developed their own countries at the expense of their African colonies.

With Britain's entry into Zanzibar to 'protect' her British Indian subjects, Indians became once more 'subjects' of Britain in a country whose development and rise to prominence was entirely due to their own efforts.

Chapter 5

Indians in Zanzibar

> **As important as the Arabs were the Indian residents in Zanzibar and the coast were perhaps more important, since almost the whole commercial and financial business on which the prosperity of Arab East Africa depended, was in their hands.**
> (Professor R. Coupland In *The Exploitation of East Africa, 1865-1890: The Slave Trade and the Scramble*, 1939).

Indians and Arabs are among the oldest visitors to Zanzibar resulting from the centuries-old trading relations with Cutch, Kathiawar and the Malabar coasts of India.

It was the Indians who opened the interior of East Africa to trade and settlement through their initiative and enterprise. Less numerous than the Arabs but with economic importance out of proportion to their number, were the Indian residents of Zanzibar. A considerable number of Indians came to Zanzibar in Seyyid Said's reign, from 200 in 1819 to 5,000 in 1844 and 6,000 in 1859.

When the Arab ruler of Oman, Seyyid Said, moved his capital from Muscat to Zanzibar in 1840 he encouraged the Indians residing in Muscat to join him as financial advisers for economic reasons and partly as a means of marketing the clove and coconut production of the islands of Zanzibar and Pemba. They never considered themselves the Sultan's subjects, they never even took their families to Africa. Unlike the Arabs the Indians did not have to settle on the Swahili coast, Zanzibar was still treated as an outpost of India by the Indians. It was only in 1861 following the death of Seyyid Said in 1856 and the succession dispute that followed, that they were forced to make a decision to consider Zanzibar as their home. It was not really a hard decision to make, for they were already familiar with their new home for centuries through trade.

From their small beginnings as seasonal traders the Indians developed a vast network of commerce throughout the region. This went from a sporadic commercial contact of the early years to a more regular and committed association in the later years. The wealthier Indians were merchants, money lenders and bankers, the less wealthy became craftsmen.

The Hindus came from Cutch, Surat and Bombay and belonged to the Bhatia and Bania sects. From 1830 the Indian Muslims included Khojas and Bohoras, those who came from Jamnagar usually returned to India. In the 19th century the Indians played a substantial role in the economic and political life of Zanzibar.

In 1591 in the reign of Queen Elizabeth I, the British ship Edward Bonaventure visited the East African coast but did not touch Zanzibar. At that time direct voyages were made from Sofala or Madagascar, straight to India. The first recorded visit of the British to Zanzibar was in 1799 when two British ships, Leopard and Orestes arrived in Zanzibar. Lt. Bissel of the Leopard reported that he saw Zanzibar town dotted with stone houses belonging to Indian merchants and wealthier Arabs.

The next more significant visit to Zanzibar was that of the East India Company cruises under the command of Capt. Smee in 1811, as a Bombay Government representative to investigate trade possibilities. As far as anyone knows this was the first time that the British Indian Government had taken any interest in the activities of their subjects in Africa. Smee reported that the wealthy Hindu traders held the best part of the trade in their hands much to the envy of the Omani Arabs. Also, that there was considerable trade between Africa, and Bombay and Surat.

Fearing the growing Arab influence in Zanzibar during Queen Victoria's reign it was decided to entrust British interests in Zanzibar to a qualified officer. Accordingly the first British Consulate was opened in Zanzibar in 1841 'to protect the interests of their Indian subjects' who were already there long before the British had heard of Africa. Capt. Atkins Hamerton of the British Indian army, an Irishman, was appointed the first British Consul to Zanzibar.

Relations between Indians and Arabs and the Government of His Highness the Sultan of Zanzibar were those of a happy family, at least on the surface, thanks to Sultan Seyyid Said's efforts. Indians held with distinction important positions as heads of departments in the Zanzibar Government. All that changed after the opening of the British Consulate. Now even unimportant posts were filled by Europeans, which entailed unnecessary financial burdens on the taxpayer, mainly the Indian merchant. After the 1918 war European countries lowered their taxes but the reverse happened in Zanzibar. In 1927 European salaries were raised by 40%, Indians' by 15%. Import duty was raised from 10% to 15%.

Despite the disadvantages Indian capital investment in Zanzibar steadily increased during the 19th century. In 1873 it was not less than £1,600,000. Apart from the important role in the wholesale and distribution trade in Zanzibar some of the leading Indian traders also provided the main banking and financial services available in Zanzibar. Capt. Hamerton acknowledged:

> The best and only certain way of obtaining a supply of cash for immediate service is by getting it from the Customs Master, Jairam Sewji even to the extent of $5,000.

Acting as bankers to agriculturists often in risky and unsecured positions, unarmed and without state protection, Indian shop keepers performed an important function of supplying the African with the necessities of life and raising their standard of living by introducing them to imported products. They contributed to the economic development of the country by linking Zanzibar to the outside world through trade.

The spectacular increase in trading between 1820 and 1850 was not purely Indo-Arab. The coastal Swahili may have led the caravans but the guides were the Nyamwezi of western Tanganyika. Many of the trade routes which the Arabs used were in fact those of the Nyamwezi and other African traders such as the Kamba and Yao who had already developed routes in Buganda, Uganda and Katanga in Congo. Indian capital financed thousands of pounds worth of trade goods to the interior, waiting for even a year or more till the caravans returned with African produce they could sell to the Europeans.

In 1857 Burton visited Zanzibar, he recorded his impressions of Indians numbering about 6,000 at the time:

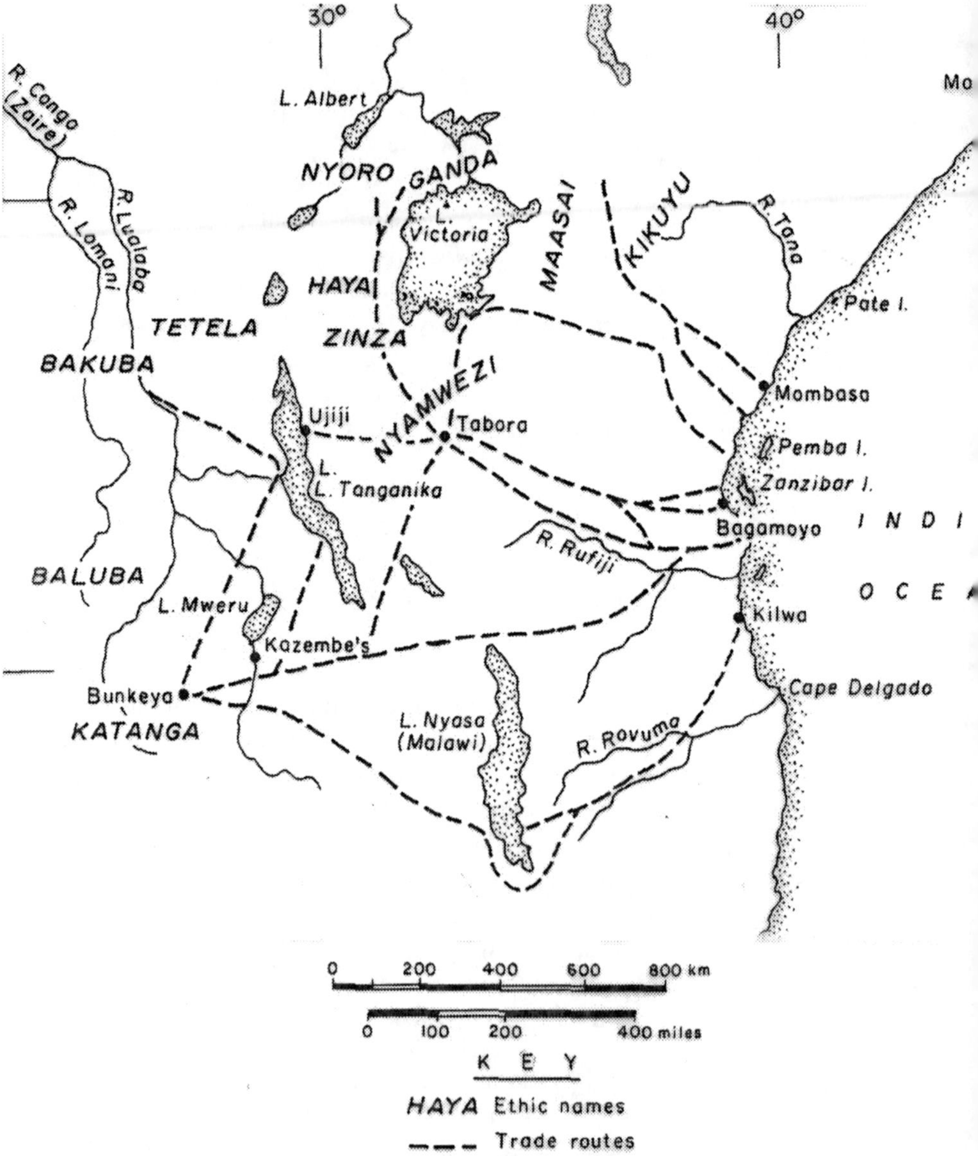

Map: Early trade routes in middle Africa
Source: The Making of Modern Africa by A.E. Afigbo pp. 323

> During the last few years the number of Indian settlers has increased. They obtain possessions from the Arabs by purchase or mortgage of landed estates. Almost all foreign trade passes through their hands. They are the principle artisans and they extend as far as Mozambique, Madagascar and the Comoros Islands. They own stone houses and large plantations. Those in Zanzibar are not anxious to display their wealth. These banyans will buy up the entire cargoes of American and Hamburg ships. Ivory from the interior is consigned to them, they purchase the copal from native traders.

Indian traders had a major share in marketing 60% of the copra and all of the clove crop produced in Zanzibar. Indian banks financed the caravans into the interior of Africa, offering credit. The flow of trade to and from India was in Indian ships, two thirds of which went to Europe and America.
Frere remarked to Granville:

> Europeans, Americans and Swahili trade and make a profit but the one link in this chain is the Indian.

It was a trade built on the long established pattern of Indian goods for African produce carried out entirely by dhow. Indian firms imported traditional Indian goods, cotton cloths, plain and indigo dyed, hardware, metal ware, grain, spices and beads from Surat in Gujerat for the markets of East Africa. These goods were exchanged for ivory, hides, horn, cloves and copra, gums (copal and arabic), dyeing drugs, rhinoceros horn, hippopotamus tusks, and a variety of parrots and ebony from Madagascar. Other imports consisted of dates and salt fish from Oman.

Zanzibar itself contributed little to this trade except for a very considerable and very valuable export of cloves. The Indian firms' representatives all along the East African coast obtained goods from French, German and American merchants who required gum copal, ivory and hides in exchange. Even passengers travelling from India to Zanzibar for the first time came on board the dhow with bundles of cloth, spices and sundry merchandise to exchange for East African products.

It is also through Indians' active help that European explorers like Burton, Speke, Grant, Stanley and even Dr. Livingstone and others were able to pursue their adventures. Indian traders acted as 'load bankers' to explorers. Burton and Speke owed Ladha Damji, Sewji's agent and banker in Pangani $26,000 for equipment. Damji also helped equip Livingstone's expeditions contracting to forward additional supplies to the interior. Burton writes:

> They are especially powerful to forward the discoverer. They can cash drafts in Zanzibar, Mandavi and Bombay. Provide outfits, guards and pagazis (porters) who are their employees. From the time of arrival, to the journey into the interior and back requires the active cooperation of the Indians.

Explorers spoke of Indian hospitality both in Zanzibar and the coastal settlements. Until they left, Indians treated them with their traditional hospitality, providing them with information on the region and the people of the area of exploration. Ladha Damji provided them with all that they needed for their journey. In 1860 Dr. Roscher an explorer, travelled on foot to the Rufiji River. He recorded Indian settlements all along the way and spoke of their great hospitality.

By 1870 there were 3,396 Khoja Muslims who came from Cutch and had adopted the Swahili language. Khojas who came from Gujerat had interests in China, Japan, South East Asia, the Arabian Peninsula and Muscat. Bhatias had a strong foothold in Bombay with operations in the Red Sea ports, Persian Gulf, China, Japan and Zanzibar. Vanias were bankers, money-changers and moneylenders. They operated commodity markets with close connections in Burma (now Myanmar), Persian Gulf, Muscat and Zanzibar. Bohoras were tinsmiths, locksmiths and ironmongers, they did not participate in foreign trade at this time. The Suni Memons were not an economically important group. Goans were clerks, accountants, chefs, cobblers, tailors and government employees.

When John Kirk arrived in Zanzibar in 1866 to take up his duties as advisor to the Sultan of Zanzibar, there were five or six thousand Indians residing in Zanzibar as well as at the coastal towns on the mainland and at the trade posts in the interior. Of these 3,666 came from British India and the rest from Cutch and Kathiawar, subjects of the Rao (Ruler) of Cutch. Burton admitted that the merchants par excellence were the Bhatias or Cutchi *banyans*. From the beginning of the 19th century the monopoly of *sherraf* (banker) fell into the hands of the Bhatia clan due to the inability of the Arabs to manage the business of banking. The Bhatias, a merchant Hindu community from Gujerat, dominated trade in Zanzibar. They outshone other communities through their business acumen and frugality of lifestyle. They have the longest known history in Kenya and in East Africa in general. (Samson, 1993).

When the Portuguese arrived at the East African coast in 1498 it was known as the Zenj (black) Empire. Among the coastal settlements they found Kilwa a well laid out town humming with trading activity and an Arab Sultan already in residence. Duarte Barbosa a Portuguese official describes Kilwa Island as having stone and mortar houses, with well carved wooden doors 'having excellent joinery'. The women wore gold chains and bracelets. Zanzibar came into prominence much later but it retains its importance to this day thanks to the Indians.

The following is an Extract from *Chronicles of the Indian Societies of Zanzibar* by the chronicler Hindu Sheth.

> As far as I remember two Bhatias were the first Hindus to settle in Zanzibar, Visanji Haridas Bhimani and Sivji Topan. They came with Sultan Seyyid Said of Zanzibar from Muscat where the Bhatias were already settled. But even before them came Madhavji Topan, Sivji Topan's brother who came from India, penniless.
>
> Sivji Topan (perhaps not related to Tharia Topan) persuaded the Sultan to give him the Ijaro of the Zanzibar Customs [to farm]. On sale of some ivory for cash Topan got the contract. Bhimani was the Sultan's first Treasurer. His Indian dhows brought merchandise, cloth from Cutch, from Muscat salt fish and dates and

earthenware pots.

Then the Hindus began to increase. Other Bhatias and Hindus of other sects all from Cutch, although now we have Hindus from Cutch, Kathiawar and Gujerat proper, all Gujerati-speaking. Zanzibar was then known as 'Sual'(coast). And the Indians were known as Sual'i (people living in Sual). Thus the Hon. Bar-at-law, Member of Leg. Co. (Legislative Council) Khimjibhai K. Sualy is to be traced to them.

Rise of Jairam Sewji. The Sultan was again in need of a large sum of money which Bhimani could not raise but Jairam Sivji, son of Sivji Topan could. This made a favourable impression so that in time he was handed over the Customs Office on condition of his agreeing to pay the Sultan a certain sum, the rest being his. [Jairam Sewji paid the Sultan $310,000 per year]. This made Sewji the most important person in Zanzibar and great was his influence as well. He was also the chief supplier to the Sultan.

Curiously the Hindus did not bring their women here for a long time. The first woman to come in 1882/83 was of the Vania community, the wife of Kurverji Padamsi a clerk (mehta) of a famous Ismaili Khoja merchant, Fazal Essa. Sultan Bargash gave her Rs 250 as a reward.

Jairam Sewji used to invite Sultan Bargash to the Diwali celebrations in his office. He (Bargash) went with all his entourage and expected the British and non-British to attend. On that day new account books were opened. On the next Padwa, European Consuls visited Jairam Sewji. The next day Chand, the Bhatias and Hindu businessmen visited Sewji. Jairam Sewji was banker to many European, Arab and Indian business houses.

Sewji was (1) Chief of Customs (2) Port Officer (3) Banker of State and Business. Cash was counted by weight. Sewji also loaned money to merchants to import goods. He had officers in Lamu, Mombasa, Kismayu, Bagamoyo, Dar es Salaam and Mogadishu. A Pass was issued in Zanzibar, on presentation of which any of the subordinate Customs Officers were exempt from tax. Mr. Popat Virji was in charge of issuing these Passes. The Customs [collection] was in the name of Jairam Sewji for nearly 60 years.

In 1878/79 the Sultan put the Customs in the hands of a very famous Indian Tharia Topan, the most influential leader of the Ismaili community. In 1882/83 it went back to Jairam Sewji. Sewji made trade in Zanzibar which had been negligible, but in time became so great as to make Zanzibar an entrepôt of the whole of the East African region. In 1886 the Customs House went to Nasser Lilani, an eminent Khoja.

The Ijaro or Customs Collection

It is the Indian banker who supplied the larger part of the capital available for business and to whom even the white settlers have not hesitated to go for financial aid. The Indian was here before the British official.
(Winston Churchill, 1908).

The most significant economic factor in the history of Zanzibar's development was the place the Indian held of Controller of Zanzibar Customs in the Sultan's Government; a vital post in the economic life of the island. The Ijarah or lease, was for five years and entailed a complete monopoly of customs collection associated with the dhow trade from Kilwa to Mogadishu. The position of Customs Collector was farmed out to the highest bidder for five years. The Zanzibar post was the most

important; the lesser posts went to assistants.
(*Samachar - Silver Jubilee*, 1929)

Below is a list of Customs Collectors from 1828 to 1892

1828 Sivji Topan was appointed the first Customs Collector by Sultan Seyyid Said, Visanji Haridas Bhimani was the Sultan's first Treasurer

1833 The Indian firm of Wat Bhima was appointed to the post of Collector of Customs for Zanzibar. Earlier they held a similar position in Mombasa

1835 Five years before Seyyid Said moved to Zanzibar Jairam Sewji was honoured with three positions:
(1) Collector of Customs.
(2) Chief Officer of the Port of Zanzibar.
(3) State Banker.
As Chief Officer of the Port, all dhows had to report to Sewji on arrival and take a permit on departure.
As State Banker Sewji lent large sums of money to Europeans, Arabs and Indians; provided financial support for State projects and trading firms. He also assisted new arrivals from India and Asia and the destitute.
Sewji held this position until 1886.

1840 Seyyid Said appointed Madhovji Topan, a Bhatia, to the customs collection. At this time the Sultan's dominions included Zanzibar, Pemba, Malindi, Kilwa, Mombasa, Bagamoyo, Tanga and other smaller ports along the East African coast.
On the death of Madhovji Topan, Ibji Shivji took over the Customs.

1843-53 The Zanzibar Customs was bought by Jairam Sewji and managed by the well-known Ladha Damji.

1856 Seyyid Majid succeeded Seyyid Said. He gave the Customs to Ladha Damji who was Sewji's agent. He was not only the Customs Master but also Treasurer of the Salote of Zanzibar.

1886 The Customs House was managed by Nasser Lilani an eminent Khoja.

1892 The British East India Company took over the Sultan's customs collection.

In 1873 Sir Bartle Frere in a letter to Lord Granville recommended the 'take charge' of the Sultan's Customs Houses managed by Indian Officials. Thus the British were casting covetous eyes on a lucrative revenue. So Sir Gerald Portal with a stroke of the pen ousted the Indians from the sphere of the Customs and the British East India Company stepped in.

From 1826 to 1892 the customs collection was managed by Indians. The Zanzibar commercial empire that emerged during the 19th century and encompassed much of eastern Africa can be attributed to the financial and political administration of the Customs Master Jairam Sewji.

The Sultan had a number of Hakims (Governors) on the mainland in Dar es Salaam and other smaller ports, to collect customs duty, but the informal system suffered from competition between the merchant class from the coast and inland. At the coast was the powerful group of financiers who were turned into instruments of British domination.

The Clove Growers' Association

Indians lived in harmony with Arabs and Africans. They held high offices of state in the Sultan's employment as well as in the Colonial Administration. The rise of some Indians to positions of trust and eminence in Zanzibar exposed them to envy, criticism and increasing scrutiny.

The most important crop of Zanzibar was cloves. Originally Arabs enjoyed the monopoly in the clove trade. But they soon got into financial problems through their lavish living and improvident spending, so that their plantations were mortgaged to Indian moneylenders who ended up by owning the plantation as a result of defaulting on the mortgage payments. Indians built up a flourishing trade in cloves.

The declining Arab monopoly induced the Zanzibar Government to set up a Commission in 1923 under M.H.R. Crofton to inquire into the setback for Arab clove growers. Messrs. Bartlett and Last accused the Indian moneylenders of using agriculture to exploit and impoverish the Arabs.

In 1927 the Zanzibar Government introduced a Clove Growers' Association (C.G.A.). The Association was formed to finance the clove growers and to stabilize labour rates with a view to eliminating ruinous private speculation and securing stable markets abroad.

The Clove Growers' Association (C.G.A.) Decree.

Terms of Reference:

1. A Decree created a Board consisting of not more than seven members appointed by the British Resident.
2. The Association was exempt from any fee in respect of its undertakings, e.g. Stamp Duty, Registration fees, etc.
3. Operations were financed by a levy on all cloves exported from the Protectorate.
4. The Association was entitled to deal in and export agricultural produce.

By 1933 conditions did not improve for the Arab clove growers. The 1934 Report by Crofton, Bartlett and Last prompted the Zanzibar Government to take measures towards safeguarding the interests of the Arab and African clove growers.

Consequently a number of Decrees against the interests of Indians were introduced in 1934, they were:

1. The Alienation of Land Decree.
   Restriction on Alienation of agricultural land belonging to Arabs or Africans, the intention being to place a ban on Indians acquiring any more land and forbidding them to bid for or acquire property already mortgaged to them.
2. Mortgage (Settlement & Redemption) Loan Decree.
   By this Decree the main intention of the Government was to give relief to the debtor (Arab) and not the creditor (Indian). Magistrates were allowed to set aside previous voluntary agreements made between debtor and creditor. Section 5 of the Bill compelled the creditor to apply for repayment within three months or lose the money.
3. The Clove Exporters' Decree.
   This Decree provided that:
   (a) No person might export cloves from the Protectorate unless he obtained a license from the Board of the C.G.A. at a cost of Rs.5,000 - not transferable without consent of the Board.
   (b) Warehouses were to be licensed. The Board was allowed to enter, examine books and registers and remove documents.
   (c) The British Resident could restrict the number of Export Licenses if necessary.

4. The Adulteration of Produce Decree.
   The introduction of a system of grading for the export of cloves, prohibited the export of the produce unless 'passed by inspection, grading and branding'. Inspectors were empowered to enter ware houses at any 'reasonable' time for inspection and even order removal of the produce from the place of inspection.

The Decrees also provided for penal clauses specifying offences and recommending punishment.

At the request of the Indian clove traders who stood to lose from the operations of the C.G.A., Mr. B.H. Binder was appointed by the Secretary of State for the Colonies to conduct an inquiry into its operations with a view to making modifications. Mr. Binder instead gave C.G.A. new and wider powers by recommending:

1 That Government issued C.G.A. only, with a license to buy and receive deposits of cloves.
2 Merchants had to buy cloves from a licensed vendor, namely the C.G.A.
3 That the C.G.A. was made a Government Department trading with public funds.

The President of the Indian National Association, Zanzibar, Mr. Tayabali Esmailjee Jivanji said:

> The clove industry is a hundred years old . . . Binder had not considered the past history of the clove industry, had he done so he would have realized that it was the Indian merchants who had brought the industry to its present position of commanding world markets and being the major suppliers and consumers. . .

Indians in the clove industry faced a serious situation as a result of the enactment of the various legislation aimed at destroying their economic life. In 1934 the Government of India dispatched one of its most trusted persons Mr. K.P.S. Menon, I.C.S., to inquire into the effect and reactions of the Indians concerned with the clove trade in Zanzibar. Mr. Menon later went to Kenya and Uganda, as Indians there were in trouble as well.

In August 1934 Mr. Menon wrote, 'When I arrived in Zanzibar I found the Indian community in a state of panic. This was partly due to the manner in which the legislation was carried out. June 16th 1934 the Bills were published, June 30th (1934) they became Decrees.' Menon's Report in brief:

> Congress supports the Indian community in Zanzibar in its just struggle against the clove legislation established by the Government to monopolize the internal and external clove trade in Zanzibar under the misnomer of Clove Growers' Association, aimed at eliminating the Indian community's clove trade.
>
> The Association composed of three members has no clove growers on the Board. The Association collects Rs 262,500 per year in levies yet pays no fees.
>
> The Decree concerning grading and adulteration authorizes the Association to order the removal of such produce from the warehouse - where to?

Menon's Report furnished prices of cloves between 1895-96 and 1933-34:

> If the plantations were mortgaged to Indians at this time as Hamerton alleged then the increased price on the world market and the consequent prosperity to Zanzibar was as a result of Indian labour and capital.

Dr. Charlesworth of Charlesworth, Pilling & Co. who lived in Zanzibar for twenty years said:

> The former great prosperity of Zanzibar was founded on the practical monopoly . . . from Guardifui to Beira . . . and created by the enterprise and intelligence of the Indian community in Zanzibar.

British Imperialism in Zanzibar

The following list traces the history of British Imperialism in Zanzibar.

1822, Sept.	Morseby Treaty prohibiting the sale of slaves from Seyyid Said's dominions to Christian countries.
1833, May 2	Treaty for the suppression of the Slave Trade.
1833, Sept. 21	Commercial Treaty between US Special Agent Edmund Roberts and Seyyid Said in Muscat
1839, May 31	Signing of Commercial Convention between Seyyid Said and Capt. Cogan of Britain in Muscat.
1841, May 4	Capt. Atkins Hamerton of the Indian Army appointed Her Majesty's Consul in Zanzibar.
1858	Hamerton is succeeded by Col. Christopher Rigby as Consul.
1859, June	Treaty of Commerce between Zanzibar and the Hanseatic (Medieval political and commercial league of German towns) Republic.
1866	Sir John Kirk becomes Adviser to the Sultan of Zanzibar.
1866, April	Lord Canning, Governor General of India declares the Imamate of Oman separate from the Sultanate of Zanzibar under the Canning Award.
1870, Jan. 5	Sir John Kirk appointed Her Majesty's Agent and Consul-General at Zanzibar.
1872	Sir Bartle Frere in a letter to Lord Grenville recommends the 'take charge' of the Sultan's Customs Houses managed by Indians.
1872, Nov.	Sir Bartle Frere appointed Special Envoy to Zanzibar and Muscat.
1873	Sir Bartle Frere appointed Special Commissioner to negotiate with Seyyid Bargash to forbid the export of slaves from his dominions.
1873	The jurisdiction over British subjects moved from the Government of India to the Imperial British Government.
1873, June 5	Seyyid Bargash signs a Treaty banning the movement of slaves by sea and closing the slave markets.
1879, Aug. 25	Commercial Treaty between Portugal and Zanzibar.
1884	German Flag first raised in Zanzibar.

1885	Formation of the Imperial British East Africa Company (I.B.E.A.C.).
1885, May 28	Commercial Treaties between Italy and Zanzibar.
1885, May 30	Commercial Conventions between Belgium and Zanzibar.
1886-1898	Sir John Kirk appointed Consul-General and Adviser to the Sultan of Zanzibar.
1887, Aug. 11	Commercial Convention between Austria and Zanzibar.
1890, June 14	Agreement between Zanzibar and Great Britain in respect of making Zanzibar a British Protectorate.
1892	The British Government appoints Sir Gerald Portal Consul-General in Zanzibar.
1892	The British East Africa Co. takes over the Sultan's Customs Houses from the Indians.
1894	Sultan Seyyid Hamoud signs a Decree on the gradual suppression of the Slave Trade.
1896, Aug. 27	British fleet bombards Zanzibar causing much damage to the House of Wonders.
1896	Zanzibar declared a British Protectorate.
1897	Treaty abolishing the legal status of slaves in Zanzibar.
1897, April	Slavery finally and totally abolished in Zanzibar.
1908, Jan.	The silver Rupee of British India made legal tender in Zanzibar at Rs 15.00 per British £ because of the close ties with India.

Chapter 6

Indians in Tanganyika and Uganda

INDIANS IN TANGANYIKA

Indian trade, enterprise and emigration require a suitable outlet. We do not naturally desire to see all the Indian enterprise in Eastern Africa sheltered by a flag that is not British.
(Sir Harry Johnston, 1901)

The colonization of East Africa by Germany was as unique as the colonization of British East Africa, by Britain. Carl Peters and a group of adventurers, thrusters, orators and imperialists, whose avowed object was to provide Germany with overseas territories travelled from Europe in disguise. This group of young Germans arrived in Zanzibar in November 1844 and set off for the interior of Africa. They returned six weeks later having made a number of 'treaties' with African Chiefs.

On his return to Berlin, Peters had no difficulty in obtaining Kaiser Bismarck's support for the 'treaties'. In 1888 the Kaiser signed a Schentzbrief placing under German protection the territories whose rulers had 'ceded and offered' their domains to a German colonization society, the German Colonial Association, authorizing the Association to take over responsibility for the administration of the new Protectorate. The districts claimed by the Germans lay well inland from the coast covering east central Tanganyika, beyond the jurisdiction of the Sultan of Zanzibar.

The British Government surprisingly decided to acquiesce in the

German coup. Accordingly Sir John Kirk, Consul for Zanzibar was instructed to 'accept' the German move. Soon a German East Africa Company was set up and by 1889 a small group of Germans from the Company arrived in Dar es Salaam. By 1890 German sovereignty was complete.

In German East Africa (later Tanganyika), a fair proportion of Indians engaged in trade and commerce had already settled in Tanga, Bagamoyo, Pangani, Lindi and Dar es Salaam. Indian settlers traded mainly in sisal which in course of time became Tanganyika's main export product.

Indian immigration to Tanganyika after German occupation was a little different from their settlement in British East Africa. The Germans recognized very early, their value as traders and admitted them freely, employing them in commerce or the manufacture of goods or as craftsmen. In fact 95% of the trading community was Indian. Chief among these pioneers was Allidina Visram who had established a duka-based business there. He had about 200 dukas throughout East Africa. However the Germans met with resistance from the Africans regarding labour for agriculture. They were therefore forced to import indentured labour from India both for agriculture and for building the railway.

The Ordinance of 1908 respecting the raising of duty on industries, businesses and trade, applicable on all profits however small, had laid down reasonable profit deductions for the support of the trader and his household. The 1908 Ordinance also required traders, innkeepers, and cattle dealers to buy 'opening licenses' on new shops. There were also the small traders who penetrated the remotest areas of Tanganyika, introducing the Africans to new products as well as opportunities in trade.

Just as Indian commerce increased so did British political influence in East Africa. In 1883 the growing momentum of the 'scramble for Africa' increased. Sir John Kirk was concerned that German paramountcy in Tanganyika would enable 'a rival nation to utilize the trading capacities of our Indian subjects to advance and develop her commerce', especially as Bagamoyo was the principal port in Tanganyika for the arrival and departure of the ivory caravans with a large concentration of Indians operating from that port.

In 1883 also the 'right of the jurisdiction over British subjects in East Africa' was transferred from the British Indian Government to the Imperial British Government. Consequently the Indian bourgeoisie had to channel their interests in East Africa via the markets in the Indian Ocean. That is, all their business ventures in East Africa were no longer connected with the Bombay Government as in the past.

With British steamships taking over the transporting of trade goods all over the world, Indian monopoly of Zanzibar's transport trade gradually diminished. The British also made an agreement with the Sultan to the effect that goods carried in British ships would be free of duty, so naturally European traders preferred to use British ships. As their monopoly of the Zanzibar transport trade decreased leading Indian firms like those of Sewa Hajee Paroo and Allidina Visram moved to German East Africa on mainland Tanganyika to safeguard their business interests in East Africa. The British also minimized the role of Indians with the formation of the Imperial British East Africa Company (I.B.E.A.C.) in 1888. Indians who had long occupied posts of importance and trust in Zanzibar under the Sheikhs found their fortunes diminished, while those of the British increased. The post of Customs Collector went to the British in 1892. The I.B.E.A.C. eventually failed because it lacked the capital of the rich Indian merchants as well as their entrepreneurial experience.

With the abolition of the slave trade Arab influence and affluence in Zanzibar dwindled. The Arabs borrowed money from Indian money lenders to continue their businesses without any intention of repaying it. Indian move to German East Africa was also brought about 'by the less favourable treatment' they received from the British who took sides with the Arabs who owed them money. However there still remained considerable Indian investment in Zanzibar.

In 1892 the British called upon important Indians to make Zanzibar a commercial depôt for fear that German East Africa would capture the Indian Ocean trade, especially as there was a great concentration of Indians at ports now under German jurisdiction. The break up of the old economic system reduced the importance of Zanzibar which led to Indians transferring their businesses to mainland German East Africa where there were still fortunes to be made.

After Germany lost the First World War of 1914-1918, Tanganyika became a Trust Territory under the League of Nations. In 1921 Indians numbered 9,411 in Tanganyika. They controlled 50% of the import and 60% of the export trade.

In 1923 when the British took over the Trust Territory from the League of Nations the 1908 Ordinance regarding duty on industries, was repealed and several discriminatory tax and trading ordinances were introduced. One discriminatory law against Indians stated that accounts were to be kept in English failing which they would be translated into English at the expense of the trader. The Ordinance affected 6,000 traders. Trade licenses could be refused without giving a reason.

The British Government also forbade Africans to sell milk to Indians, which as vegetarians they consumed a lot of. Although handicapped the Indian trader of Tanganyika remained faithful to his commercial pursuits contributing to the growth of the colony. Thanks to Indian enterprise, exports of sisal rose from £1.5 million in 1938 to £56 million in 1960.

Till the early 20th century Indians were preoccupied with improving their economic interests and opportunities. In 1937 the Imperial Government reported to the League of Nations on the administration of the Tanganyika Trust Territory:

> The Indian trader has formed a link between the native purchaser and the wholesale importer. In the remote areas of the country he performs the double function of buyer and seller. Evidence shows that native and non-native trade is complementary and not antagonistic.

INDIANS IN UGANDA

> **Churchill said that India was the 'Jewel in the crown of the British Empire' while Uganda was the 'Pearl of Africa'.**
> (Bhanuben Kotecha In *On the Threshold of East Africa,* 1994.)

In Uganda as in other East African territories, Indian interests have been largely commercial. With the expansion of the Uganda Railway Indians settled in Uganda, the majority following their usual commercial pursuits. A leading Indian merchant Allidina Visram is reported to have set up trading in Uganda twenty years before the railway reached Lake Victoria. Allidina Visram, Nanji Kalidas Mehta and Vithaldas Hardas were among the first to transport goods to Uganda using headload caravans. The Indian was not confined to the urban centers alone but penetrated remote areas as well. Ingrams in his *Study on Uganda* was impressed at the variety of goods sold in a small Indian duka including 'Pepsi'.

Those Indians who went into agriculture held 62,440 acres of agricultural land, which included two large sugarcane plantations producing 5,000 tons of white sugar per year. Indians also introduced the cotton industry in Uganda.

Allidina Visram arrived in Zanzibar from India and became a trader at the age of twelve. He began his career on the East African coast in Bagamoyo. At first he supplied porters and equipment to European explorers going inland from the coast. After 1898 his caravans went northwards from Mwanza into Uganda and then to Kisumu in Kenya. Initially he concentrated only on exporting ivory from Uganda but later he promoted the duka-based trade by being a supplier of goods to the small traders in remote areas in Uganda and elsewhere. Goods were transported by portage to places nearer the coast, and by donkey and bullock cart to more distant destinations. By 1904 he had 200 dukas in Zanzibar, Dar es Salaam, Tabora and Mwanza in Tanganyika; Mombasa and Kisumu in Kenya; Hoima in Uganda and Gondokoro in Sudan.

Allidina Visram the pioneer of organized trade was the first Indian to establish stable businesses in Uganda employing clerks and other personnel. The Africans knew him as *pagaji*. He had branches in all important centers big and small. In 1911 he arrived in Congo on foot to explore business possibilities there.

He started cotton-growing in Entebbe, Uganda, on his own 5-acre plot with seeds extracted by hand from cotton pods imported from India. In 1918 he experimented with growing sugarcane on his own land in Busoga, Uganda. His manager was a Parsee, D.F. Dastur, but his workers included Africans, Baluchis and Indians. His trading company acted as the first 'Bank of Uganda'. Beside the 200 shops throughout East Africa, Sudan and Congo, Allidina Visram's empire included Bombay and Addis Ababa, Ethiopia.

Nanji Kalidas Mehta travelled to Madagascar in 1900 most probably via Muscat, at the age of thirteen, for adventure. His father was rich but he had heard stories about adventure in Africa. His autobiography *Dream Half Expressed,* cites forty-five journeys from 1901 to 1961 between India and Africa and within Africa 'daring to go in search of trade where no white man had gone before'. Nanji Kalidas Mehta pioneered the sugar and cotton industries in Uganda which became the foremost industries in the country.

From 1920 to 1930 Nanji Kalidas Mehta of Uganda Sugar Mills and Muljibhai Madhvani of Kakira Sugar Mills bought land on which European crops had failed, to plant sugarcane. The Uganda Sugar Factory was started in 1924 in Lugazi, and the Kakira Sugar Factory was started in 1930 in Madhvaninagar outside Jinja. From 1934 to 1936, 55,000 tons of sugar was produced. Through Indian enterprise oil mills were built for crushing cottonseed. The seed at first considered waste material had become a money earner and added considerable prosperity to Uganda. The pulp was made into a seed cake rich in protein, which was exported as cattle feed as well as compost.

In 1897 Uganda published its first trade record. Imports were cotton cloths, beads, metal ware, eastern silks, linen and miscellaneous manufactured goods, traded for ivory. Up to 1902 trading consisted of bartering of goods for ivory.

In the early history of Indian enterprise in East Africa there had been relatively little contact between the African and Indian. Indians dealt with the powers that controlled the inland trade routes. They had not concerned themselves with the production of goods, they merely financed their collection and were responsible for the sale and distribution. But as they went inland they encountered competition from the highly materialistic Baganda who entered the economic market with zeal, especially in the cotton industry which the Indians had introduced into Uganda. The Indian monopoly on cotton growing was gradually taken over when the Baganda entered the trade.

The Indian population continued to increase steadily and by 1911 Indians numbered 10,651. They did not all belong exclusively to the trading community. The Protectorate depended on Indian clerks, artisans and craftsmen. Very few engaged in agriculture due to the British policy of European monopoly in owning agricultural land. However there was a substantial group of cotton and sugarcane planters whose crops became an integral part of the Protectorate's export products.

In 1898 Manchester in England tried to produce a cotton cloth suited to the African need. The *Uganda Gazette* of 4, October 1899 advertised its first list of imported goods; cheap looking-glasses, beads, brassware, clocks and cheap jewelry. Up to about 1911 the principal imports were cotton goods, umbrellas, soaps, perfumes, corrugated iron sheets, beads, crockery and glassware. By 1912 beads ceased to be an import item as they were being made by Africans in Zimbabwe, a craft taught by the Indians. At this time also the Indian Rs 5.00 denomination was accepted as currency. The approach of the railway to Uganda, 1902-03 heralded the real import trade into Uganda. Sir Harry Johnston, Commissioner 1899-1901, expressed 'thanks to British Indian enterprise. No important center of European settlement is without its well appointed store.' He made strong recommendation for expansion of British Indian commerce, enterprise and immigration.

By 1921 the number of Indians had greatly increased. Cotton mills were established in Uganda between 1914 and 1925. Indians developed the cotton industry, owning the largest number of cotton gins. Indians also distributed 'American' upland cotton seed to the Africans who eventually took over the cotton plantations, while the Indians concentrated on the ginning, marketing and export trade.

Immediately the cotton crop appeared on the Uganda market the firm of Narandas Rajaram started producing cotton cloth with a Mr. Folks as manager. The other manufacturer of cotton cloth was Mangaldas Khandwala. Up to about 1920 the leading firms in Uganda were of Allidina Visram, Narandas Rajaram, Kenya General Agency, Devchand Purshottam & Co. and Vithaldas & Co.

The producers paid large sums of money in tax and employed 3,000 workers. They built schools, hospitals and sports facilities for the workforce. Laljibhai Vadera and Devjibhai Hindocha shared the cost of educating President Milton Obote, although his father was a chief. When Burton needed to exchange English currency into other currencies, he used Alladina's 'bank'. Burton was delighted to find that be had made a 'small profit' in the transaction.

The impact of the world economy had without doubt hit Uganda with the building of the Uganda Railway from Mombasa to Kisumu on Lake Victoria in 1901. The British Government was anxious to generate traffic for its expensive railway by exporting the cotton crop and creating taxable income. According to Mr. Ramachandani in *India and Africa* (1980) the British Government of Uganda depended considerably on Indian skills, capital and enterprise for the development of the territory and the Indians although a small community paid considerable sums of money in taxes. Exports rose from £ 43,000 in 1908 to £ 307,000 in 1910. Narandas Rajaram of Bombay marketed Uganda cotton to the Bombay market.

> The dukawalla or petty shopkeeper has carried his wares far and wide into remote areas and has introduced the products of European industry among the most primitive tribes. By increasing their wants he has created an incentive to effort and thus sown the first seeds of economic progress. The Indian trader has performed another useful function in marketing the products of native agriculture. For instance the greater part of the valuable cotton crop of Uganda is handled by Indian buyers and their activities have undoubtedly stimulated the speed of cotton collection. The middleman (Indian) is a necessary link in the chain of distribution. The European cannot afford to trade on the small scale and with the small margin of profit on which the Indian subsists.
> (Report to the Hilton Young Commission, 1927)

The other indispensible function of the Indian was the marketing of 'native' products. The greater part of the cotton grown by the Baganda was handled by Indians, which stimulated the growing of cotton. The British considered Indian middlemen a necessary link in the chain of distribution.

Again in 1928 the Hilton Young Commission reported that Indian ability and skill were indispensable to the country.

> We have heard complaints of unfair dealings by Indian traders both as buyers and sellers. Such charges are brought against middlemen all over the world. Indian middlemen are doing useful work for which no other agency is at present available.
> (Sir E. Hilton Young, 1928)

Indians in Uganda in 1948, excluding a small number of Goans from Portuguese India, numbered 33,767, a striking increase since 1921. The majority were engaged in trade. In 1948 Indians owned 90% of the cotton gins and 60% of the cotton lint was shipped to India. The British tried to break the monopoly the Indians enjoyed in the cotton industry. Consequently the British Cotton Growing Association was formed 'to promote the cotton grown in the British Empire and to cut dependence on foreign sources'. Even Missionaries got involved in the marketing of cotton through the Uganda Company Ltd., a commercial firm set up for ginning and shipping cotton.

Although Indians had no political aspirations, in 1919 in order to protect their commercial interests and capital outlay in Uganda, they formed the Central Council of Indian Associations in Kampala, Jinja and Mbale.

> Some came for adventure some out of curiosity, but the primary hope in all groups was economic prosperity. (Gregory, 1993).

Chapter 7

Indians in Kenya

> **Indians of all people should not forget their history, theirs is much greater than ours with periods of splendid greatness, nor however should we forget it. If we opened Kenya to them, we could not have made her what she is, without them.**
> (Lord Altrinham, formerly Sir Edward Grigg, 1955. Governor of Kenya 1925-1931)

Indians first came to Kenya as traders and much later as settlers. This was largely in the unrecorded past of the history of the East African coast. Indian contact began with voluntary exchange of goods, its regularity was dependent upon the willingness of the Africans to exchange their surplus products for Indian goods. The trade did not destroy the economic organization of pre-capitalist Kenya, instead it introduced welcome changes in the subsistence economy. Subsistence farmers tried to produce more to exchange for foreign products.

From the 15th to the 19th centuries with the first European contact with East Africa, trade became 'unvoluntary' (Gupta, 1981). The increased trade in slaves and ivory upset the economy without introducing new means of production. The only advantage was that the large scale production for export that resulted from the coming of the Europeans, required transportation by railway and a port at Mombasa, not only for exporting goods but also for administrative purposes.

Although Indians began visiting East Africa centuries before the Europeans, it was only with the opening of the British Consulate in Zanzibar in 1841 that British Indian merchants were helped in their 'legitimate commerce' in addition to paving the way for other immigrants.

The Indian trader sought the protection of the British Empire, for although they had operated independently for many centuries, circumstances were changing in the perception of trade, especially with so many western traders entering the field. The British Indian Government also realized the importance of the Indian trader who came with money and business acumen. The Indians were mostly independent financiers linked with the East African coast through trade, kinship and communal ties (Seidenberg, 1996). Later, with the expansion of British hegemony over the Kenyan coast they arrived in significant numbers. By 1896 British rule was firmly established in British East Africa (later Kenya).

Immigration of Indians to British East Africa actually started on a large scale only when work on the Uganda Railway began in 1895. As the railway progressed, an Indian support community formed to cater for the special needs of the labourers in foods and vegetables. After they were joined by their families trade flourished so that they were able to supply even the European community with goods of their culture and needs. It would be misleading to assume that Indians targeted their trade towards an European clientele only. The Indian trader looked for his customers wherever he could find them and endured much hardship to meet supply and demand.

About this time also Gujerati and Cutchi speaking Bohora Muslims and some of the trade oriented Bhatia community from Bombay who had settled in Zanzibar and Dar es Salaam and along the coastal towns for generations, moved their businesses to Mombasa. Prominent among those who had amassed wealth in Zanzibar, now moving to British East Africa was A.M. Jeevanjee (Mangat,1969), a ship owner and General Merchant who already had commercial interests in Karachi, Sindh and Australia.

In 1890 A.M. Jeevanjee obtained a contract to import labourers, artisans, stevedores and builders for the British Government, to work at the port of Mombasa. In 1896 Jeevanee's firm was again hired by the Uganda Railway to recruit Indian construction workers to erect temporary buildings, rock cuttings and earthworks. In 1898 he made a profitable agreement with the Railway to supply provisions to the workers at a concession. In 1899 he obtained a contract to build a house for John Ainsworth a Government official, just in time to get a foothold in Nairobi (Mangat, 1969). In 1901 A.M. Jeevanjee started a weekly in Mombasa, the *African Standard*. In 1905 it was bought by a European. The newspaper was renamed the *East African Standard* and was used to voice ideas and policies of Lord Delamere and Colonel Grogan.

The majority of merchants who ventured into the interior were however petty traders who spread along the advancing railway line establishing small shops and administrative posts, helping the change from a barter-based economy to a money-based economy. The ancient Indian trade connection with East Africa was marked by the use of Indian coinage in 1908 and by the extension of British law in the form of Indian Codes. Since a large part of the trade was with India and Indian merchants, the East African territories adopted the rupee currency. This irked the white settlers and friction developed between Europeans and Indians. Trading and selling became the socio-economic identification of the Indian *dukawallah*.

After the completion of the railway project the majority of the coolies brought in to build the Uganda Railway returned to India. Some of those who opted to remain in British East Africa became market gardeners. They grew cotton, sugarcane and rice, linseed and various tropical fruits and vegetables near the Kibos River in Kavirondo. Sir Harry Johnston remarked:

> If we settle Indian farmers on either side of the railway line, the ensuing profit from local trade and from use of the railway will make good the cost of the construction (of the railway) and the whole will become like a pleasure garden.

Those who became petty traders, opened small dukas wherever they saw an opening for trade. Content with a low standard of living they traded where prospects for profit were precarious and poor. Others earned their living by becoming artisans, carpenters and stonemasons.

Most of the clerical staff that came for the building of the railway however, stayed on and were soon joined by immigrants from India seeking better economic prospects. Among these new arrivals were artisans, carpenters, stonemasons and building contractors. Quarry-masters, dealers in limestone and sandstone, barbers, cobblers, tailors and even landowners. On a professional level were barristers, lawyers and schoolteachers. Immigration of professionals in technical fields such as engineering, medicine, accounting and the legal profession were restricred by the British Administration.

The Indian population already in Kenya that had penetrated inland prior to the completion of the railway in 1898, was predominantly from Cutch and Gujerat. They were trading in Kibwezi and Machakos, and even in Nairobi in 1899. Adamjee Alibhoy established himself in Machakos in 1892 or 1893. In 1896 J. Walsh, Protector of Indian Immigrants wrote:

> . . . the number of immigrants living in the bush, cultivating, trading and living on their own resources was far greater than those contracted by the British. Whereas other 'foreign' traders received assistance from their governments, the Indians maintained themselves without Government support.

It must be emphasized here that when immigration of Indians took place at the beginning of the 20th century, it was at the invitation of the administrating power and it was to do work which the Africans were unable to do and Europeans were insufficient as well as unwilling to undertake at low wages. The Indians continued to fill this role for fifty years and in this way they have been more important than the African and European in building the country at a far greater rate and at a higher level than it would have been possible without them.

The Indian trader provided the Africans in the interior with goods they had never before encountered. The British realized that the thrifty Indian imported luxury goods like soaps, bicycles, clothing, liquor and textiles to sell at a very low profit margin. In 1910 Sir John Kirk remarked on the work of Indian traders in Nairobi:

> In fact drive away the Indians and you may as well shut up the Protectorate. It is only by means of the Indian trader that articles of European use can be obtained at moderate prices.

Gradually Indians played a crucial role in the colony's development in the early years of colonial rule by becoming the most prominent operators in trade and commerce in the colony. They laid the foundation for a retail trade and provided a basis for the currency. They were also responsible for the creation of a transportation system and for opening up trade in remote areas. Sir Winston Churchill wrote in *My African Journey*:

> It is the Indian trader who penetrating and maintaining himself in all sorts of places to which no white man would go or in which no white man would earn a living, has more than anyone else developed the beginnings of trade and opened up the first slender means of communication.

The building of the railway encouraged European colonization and settlement. Only a rare family could walk from Mombasa to Nairobi as did the McQueens in 1896. Whereas Indians had been walking all over East Africa for trade, and even after the railway was completed Indians still walked into remote areas carrying trade goods.

Even before white settlement gathered momentum Indians were already an integral part of the economic life of Kenya. The white settlers were seriously disturbed by the Indian presence. The possibility of developing an East African Protectorate as a new dominion had fired the imagination of Hugh Cholmondeley, Baron Delamere, who in 1897 had trekked from Somaliland to Lake Rudolf (now LakeTurkana) and then to Mt. Kenya and the Aberdares. A small number of Europeans and several thousand Indians were already settled there. He envisioned the East African Protectorate becoming another Union of South Africa, now stretching from the Cape of Good Hope to the Zambezi. If his dream was not realized it was because the Imperial Government could not 'ride roughshod over the interests of their British Indian subjects'.

It was about this time that European settlers began to arrive in large numbers and that created fears that the activities of the Indians would hinder the progress of the new settlers. The colonial administration being under heavy pressure from the settler community to restrict Indian immigration, was influenced by conflict of interest. Complaints first came from Lord Delamere:

> All the vegetables grown for the town is done by Indians, all the butchers are Indian, all the small country stores are kept by Indians. Thus they fill

> all the occupations and trades which would give employment to the poor white colonists arriving new in the country.

In 1897 Lord Delamere instigated the idea of the 'white highlands' and by 1905 these lands were entirely in the hands of immigrants from England and Europe, and the Dutch from South Africa. Propaganda about Indians not being able to develop the country began to appear in Government documents. Indians were allowed to farm in the low lying scrubland, sandy soil and other semi-arid parts of the country. The argument being that these climates were unhealthy for Europeans.

The East African Indians that the white settlers encountered were not the so-called coolies recruited for the building of the railway, the bulk of whom had returned to India. The white settler families were surpassed in number and in wealth by the Indian families long resident at the coast. These Indians were the commercial men or petty traders many of whose forebears had traded at the East African coast for generations, and who had financed the caravans that travelled into the interior. These Indians were traders, shopkeepers, artisans and technicians; big and small merchants who had played a vital role in the economic life of East Africa. They were Indians who had followed the railway as it advanced towards the Lake, some of whom were anxious to put down roots and acquire land. They were joined by new immigrants who rapidly moved into the interior to exploit the opportunities created by the building of the railway, filling clerical jobs, developing trade not only around railway stations but also in remote areas.

Kenya was declared a British Protectorate on July 1, 1895 under the name of British East Africa and made a Crown Colony called Kenya Colony in 1920. But the Indians had settled there long before the British came to East Africa, they had established themselves as traders, carrying out financial transactions and maintaining businesses. They had played an important role in building the railway and in financing development. Churchill in *My African Journey* said:

> It is by Indian labour that the one vital railway on which everything else depends, was constructed.

In Kenya as in all the other East African territories, Indians were attracted to trade in the early days of their settlement, but the British required service at a lower level. Those who followed trade and commerce had to contend with restrictive measures passed against them. Several discriminatory regulations were introduced against the non-white communities both Indian and African. The Kenya Marketing of Native Produce Bill of 1932 allowed the licensing authority to refuse trading licenses to Indian traders under the pretext of protecting African traders, of whom there were hardly any. This protection did not work in favour of the Africans either, because the lack of competition as well as the lack of variety of goods restricted the horizon and stunted the growth of the rural economy. Sir Harry Johnston referred to the injustices meted out by the white settlers to the Indians 'who strove before they were born to open up East Africa' by pointing out that it was the presence of the Indian trader on the East African coast which was the 'main justification for British interference in those regions'.

In the early days of colonization there was no friction between Indians and Africans as long as African advancement was not hindered by the Indian presence whether in trade or the services sector. Till the early part of the 20th century the Indians were preoccupied with improving their economic interests and opportunities. The Indian played a key role in laying the foundation of the East African economy. The Imperial Government reported that the Indian trader had formed a link between the native purchaser and the wholesale importer. In the more remote parts of the territory he had performed the double function of buyer and seller of African produce.

One activity the British encouraged was the expansion of shop-keeping and the retail trade in the countryside. They deplored over concentration of Indian shops in urban areas. Small shops were necessary for a cash economy as money was fast becoming the only medium of exchange in the increasing demand for goods.

In 1889 Indians had a small encampment in Nyrobi, a Maasai word meaning 'place of cool water'. By 1890 as the railway progressed this camp grew into a flourishing bazaar with Indian judicial legislation, 80% of the capital invested being Indian. On 16, April 1900 a Nairobi Township Committee was set up and municipal regulations were published in 1902 by Sir Charles Eliot.

Trade in Kenya was in the hands of Indians but they were unhappy with the restrictions on land ownership on racial grounds. It was the

Indians' hard earned taxes which were being used to develop the country, making European immigration possible, but they could not own agricultural land in the designated 'white highlands'. Indians saw no reason why they could not live where they chose considering it was they who 'opened up Africa.'

The Indians found an unexpected champion in Sir Frederick Jackson, Deputy Commissioner of the Protectorate, in their quest for land. He assured the Indians in a letter to the Secretary of the Indian Association dated 28, August 1902:

> You are in error in supposing that the Government has any intention of drawing a distinction between Europeans and Indians as far as rights of mining, settling and acquiring land are concerned.

Jackson issued a Government notice inviting Indian agriculturists to come to the Protectorate. Sir Charles Eliot, High Commissioner for Kenya Colony, while fully appreciating the benefits provided by Indian traders, saw possibilities of farming only on the shores of Lake Victoria or the Tana River for Indians growing cotton, sugar cane and rice, but was opposed to Indian acquisition of land in the cooler parts of Kenya. Sir Harry Johnston envisaged both European and Indian settlement, provided each played his part in the economic development of the country. But he was left in no doubt about the views of the few European settlers.

In 1904, a Mr. Winearls opened a hotel in Nairobi which became an acknowledged place for political meetings, The Norfolk Hotel. In January 1902 twenty-two Europeans met to elect a committee to encourage white settlement. The subject of their letter to Sir Charles Eliot, now Governor of Kenya was, 'Seeking Government support for white settlers in Kenya and opposition to land and labour to Indians.' These twenty-two people met in Nairobi also, to elect a committee to oppose Indian immigration described as 'detrimental to the European settlers in particular and the indigenous people in general'.

Sir Harry Johnston gave some thought to the Indian agriculturist. In January 1902 he experimented by settling a hundred Indian families on the low-lying land in Kibos. In response to the Indian demand for land they were now allowed to farm in the scrubland, sandy soil and other arid and semi-arid parts of the country like Machakos. It was also decided to give Indians land in areas which were considered unhealthy for Europeans. Accordingly in 1906 a thousand acres in Kibos and Kisumu in Nyanza, came under cultivation by Indians. The fertile soil produced maize, cotton, sugarcane, rice and Indian vegetables.

In 1905 when Indians wanted land in the 'White Highlands', they felt that it was their right to be treated equally with the white farmer. When the Aga Khan visited Kenya Colony that year the Indians asked him to use his good offices to try and convince the British Government of their right to land in the highlands. However the Aga Khan advised them not to press for land in the fertile regions but to be satisfied with land considered inferior. They had been allotted land in Machakos District which was semi-arid and unproductive. Nevertheless with irrigation the Indians produced vegetables, lentils, beans and grains. And later even an assortment of fruit to supply to Kenya Orchards Limited (KOL). Seeing this development, the white farmers including Grogan, successfully cultivated thousands of acres south of Machakos.

And as for the demand for land in the Highlands, this was met in part by Colonel Grogan himself who sold 136 acres in the Nairobi swamp area to Ahmedali Hebatullah in 1924. Hebatullah had consulted his spiritual leader in India who advised him to go ahead with the sale even though the Council had declared it an unsuitable building site.

By 1905 Indian demand for land became so insistent that a Lands Board was set up, with Lord Delamere the first leader of the settlers as President and Colonel Grogan as Member. Delamere himself secured 100,000 of the best acres in the highlands. Lord Francis Scott, Earl of Plymouth 350,000 acres, others including Grogan got more. The status quo was then legalized as Crown Land, the basic feature being the exclusion of non-Europeans. Delamere argued strongly against further immigration of Indians into Kenya 'because the relationship between white and black was complementary, but the introduction of the Indian would "put a wedge" in the relationship'. This would prevent the European from expanding and the African from rising. For the benefit of the new white farmers freehold model farms, a forestry department and mining laws 'making natives more amenable to European supervision' were passed.

The settlers were granted extensive plantations. The Kikuyu and other tribes were gradually squeezed out. The Indians sent several delegations to the Colonial Office to point out the injustice of the situation, to no avail. So determined were the white settlers to monopolize the country that when the Colonial Office proposed granting land to Indians who had been brought to build the railway, a group of ex-army officers including Generals, Majors and Captains, formed a vigilante committee to agitate for the expulsion of Indians from Kenya. The new Governor, South African born Sir Robert Coryndon, afraid of a rebellion declared 12,175 square miles in the Highlands for 29,000 Europeans; 43,000 square miles for 5,000,000 Africans. Those who could not fit into this area were allowed to live on European farms as squatters.

By the 1900s also the Civil Service in East Africa was organized on a racially determined system; the British occupying administrative positions, Goans and Indians filling skilled middle level positions. Official discrimination created a widespread sense of grievance among educated Indians. Promotion prospects were limited, lack of opportunities in the technical fields discouraged people in the engineering, accounting, medical and legal professions. However the Colonial Government had to draw on some Goan and some Indian expatriates to fill subordinate posts in the Colonial Administration. Indians occupied a peculiarly important position within the East African power structure. They knew English, understood the British administration methods and were 'satisfied with lower salaries' than British employees.

By the 1900s Indian political associations sprang up all over East Africa. Primarily Indians in all three East African territories had no political ambitions. Their only concern in political activity was because they felt the need to protect their social and economic interests, fight unjust and discriminatory laws and hostile colonial machinations which undermined their status in the country in which they had initiated so much development. Being intelligent and perceptive, they saw that the British were furthering their own interests at their expense by discrediting them in the eyes of the Arab and African.

> For such people to enter politics, bridge their communal diversities, form political organizations, was a remarkable undertaking. More remarkable is the fact that in East Africa they were to join their interests with those of the Africans and exercise an appreciable influence on the course of the colonial government. (Gregory, 1993).

The first Indian political organization in British East Africa (Kenya), was in Mombasa. The Mombasa Indian Association was started in 1900 by a businessman, L.M. Savle aided by his wife. Mr.Savle's business was that of Manufacturers' Representative. He was also described as a 'fiery Maratha' because of his elephant hunting. He was helped in his initiative by three of the wealthiest men in the country, Allidina Visram, Alibhai M. Jeevanjee and Tayabali Mulla Jeevanjee. In 1906 Allidina Visram launched a similar association in Nairobi which became more powerful than the one in Mombasa. By 1914 as Indian influence expanded, associations were formed in Kisumu, Naivasha, Eldoret and Fort Hall, (Murang'a). An umbrella body called the British East Africa Indian National Congress was formed with Mr. A. M. Jeevanjee as the first President. However the name was soon changed to East Africa Indian National Congress (EAINC).

At the first session of the British East Africa Indian National Congress in 1914, the Presidential address was given by Mr. A.M. Jeevanjee:

> The Indians were here first. Ours is the larger community . . . our industry and enterprise have built the prosperity of East Africa. We should say to the white settlers, 'this is not a white man's country, it is an Indian colony . . . you have robbed us of the fruits of our toil and industry . . .'

In 1907 A.M. Jeevanjee was appointed to the Legislative Assenbly. (presumably Legislative Assembly was an earlier name for the Legislative Council). He became the spokesman for grievances against the Indian community. His consideration was mainly for obtaining basic human rights so far denied them.

On 14, March 1914 the East Africa Indian National Congress (EAINC) was constituted with T. M. Jeevanji as President, L. M. Savle, Keshavlal Dwidedi and A. M. Jeevanjee as Founder Members, Allidina Visram and Shrinivas Thakur as members.. The EAINC was an umbrella organization covering all the Associations formed by Indians in East Africa: the Dar es Salaam Indian Association, the Central Council of Indian Associations (Uganda), the Indian National Association (Zanzibar) including all the Indian Associations in Kenya.

These leaders of the Indian community, most prominent being the Jeevanjees, organized a series of meetings to educate the Indian public by forming political organizations to create awareness of their past, and a realization of their right to certain privileges resulting from their history and achievements. 'To defend and maintain a watchful eye upon derogation of the rights enjoyed, and encroachment upon rights enjoyed from time immemorial.'

The years between the two World Wars saw the immigration of a professional class of Indians into East Africa. In Kenya there were V.V. Phadke and Cowasjee Manackji Dalal the first two to be appointed to the new Legislative Council, B.S Varma and A.B. Patel, Barristers, J.B. Pandya and Shams-ud-Deen were among other professionals. Before the 1914 war only the Jeevanjees were active in politics, after the war Indian political activity became aggressive, but the most important effect of the activity was to stimulate African awareness of their own rights (Gregory, 1993).

Political controversy dated back to the 1920s when Indians were first given representation in the Nairobi Municipal Council. At this time Indians numbered 23,000 to 10,000 Europeans. They comprised a significant third of the Kenyan population which occupied a controlling socioeconomic position between the dominant European minority and the African majority even in the 1920s. But they were restricted from owning land and forced to live segregated from other races. Consequently a crisis arose in 1920 when they wanted to buy land in the White Highlands and sought abolition of all discrimination against owning land. Indians also wished to compete on merit for positions in the Civil Service and advocated a common Voter Roll. They also protested against unreasonable taxation and on July 10, 1921 Indians declared 'No taxation without representation', which gave rise to the 'Indian Question' in February 1923.

Colonel Ewart S. Grogan of 'the only man to trek from Cape to Cairo' fame, passed through Kenya in 1899. He returned to the country in 1904 as a partner in a timber business and in his own words 'rapidly acquired considerable interests'. Grogan was preoccupied with 'The Indian Question' for the rest of his life. In 1923 he wrote an article for the *National Review* on the topic of 'The Indian Question' which he called *Logic of Facts* in which he argued that:

> No Indian ever played in Africa the part of a 'Livingstone', no Indian ever moved to tame the

> wilderness or touched African soil until some other race had imposed safe and ordered existence upon the spot.

The Indian part according to him had been purely trader and usurer and now safely ensconced as artisan so as to 'resist the employment of Africans'. He was emphatic that the Indian had contributed nothing while the European had contributed millions and the Indian had no rights 'in other people's country.' Grogan himself had managed to acquire 186,394 acres of the best land, more than any other settler including Delamere.

In 1917 the European community formulated a charge against the Indians of moral depravity.

> . . . inciters of crime and vice calculated to embitter racial feeling. Better educated Indians express seditious propaganda, non-cooperation and civil disobedience movements, 'a grave danger among ignorant races of Africa'.

It also declared that the Indian quarters had an outbreak of plague due to disregard for sanitation. J.M. Nazareth In *Brown Man, Black Country* 1981, wrote:

> The greatest triumph of European racism was the way in which it succeeded in deflecting African hostility from the European to a safely helpless scapegoat, the Indian.

The Nairobi Municipality was confronted with the impossible task of keeping clean and healthy a cosmopolitan town in the tropics on a small revenue from rates. Diseases like typhoid fever from soil contamination and malaria from inadequate drainage and overcrowding of the 'Indian bazaar' where 4,300 Indians lived on a space of seven acres, were endemic. It was a problem created by a community denied full civic rights, forbidden by law to build, own or rent property outside the town and restricted within certain areas. Indians could have business premises in any part of Nairobi but they could not live there. They had been offered a large area on the banks of the Nairobi River but it was low and unhealthy.

It was also priced too high, so the Indians refused to build there.

At a meeting of the Nairobi Town Council in 1920 Councillor J. M. Campos, the representative of the Indians gave the following statistics.

European area	2,700 acres - population 2,235 - 33 miles of road - 510 public lamps
Indian area	300 acres - population 6,589 -- 5 miles of road -- 30 public lamps

European area	Cost of building one acre plot - £ 100
Indian area	Cost of building plot 50 X 75 ft. in Grogan/River Road -- £ 65

Rates paid by Europeans	£ 4,700
Rates paid by Indians	£ 5,900

By 1923 the so-called 'Indian Question' loomed large on the political horizon. A meeting was organized on 16th and 17th September 1923, chaired by Mr. Hakisingh. The Governor Sir R. Coryndon was invited to listen to the Annual Report of the Congress protesting against the unreasonable taxation imposed on the community.

At the same time there was serious trouble in Tanganyika over the British Government's legislation to stifle the growth of business with heavy taxation. Indians there suspended business throughout Tanganyika Territory for six weeks. Through the good offices of Yusufali Karimjee some of the grievances from Zanzibar and Tanganyika were redressed and business resumed.

The Indian demand for agricultural land in Kenya alarmed the settlers and there was widespread speculation about the 'Indian Question'. In the White Paper of 1923 Lord Delamere requested the Imperial Government to 'grant Kenya self-governing status within any period of time which needed to be taken into consideration'. The British Government stated categorically that even if Indian interests were not promoted they would not be totally ignored. At the same time the British government stated that when independence was eventually granted to Kenya 'African interests would be paramount.' Representation for Indians in the Legislative Assembly of Kenya was also conceded.

Accordingly the Imperial British Government published the

Devonshire Declaration of 23, July 1923 which stated in part:

> Primarily Kenya is an African territory and His Majesty's Government think that the activities of the African natives must be paramount and should the interests of the immigrant races conflict, those of the former should prevail.

Later Colonial Secretaries emphasized that the 'immigrant races' in the Declaration referred to the Indians only, whose agitation against discriminatory legislation presumably menaced the Africans. In 1923 the British Government went on record as supporting 'native paramountcy' and the Devonshire Declaration or White Paper of 1923 as it was more commonly known, supplied a formula for the election of five Indian representatives from the communal voter roll.

However in spite of the affirmation on 'native paramountcy' Africans continued to be marginalized while being used to sideline the Indians. The Devonshire Declaration ensured short-term white supremacy but the settlers lost the battle for self-government which they had hoped for. In 1923 also, the settler community formed the African and European Trade Organization with Delamere as head, yet there was no move towards 'native paramountcy' while every move indicated leanings towards the Rhodesias and Nyasaland and strong ties with South Africa.

The struggle between the European and Indian communities in Kenya had first started in Mombasa which resulted in the notorious White Paper of 1923 which the Indians never accepted. The Devonshire Declaration of 1923, although proclaiming 'native paramountcy', made no difference in the lives and status of the Africans. Instead it emphasized the European privileged position. Indians strenuously opposed the content of the White Paper which virtually proposed self-government under white domination

The Indians held a series of meetings to point out to the Indians themselves as well as the white settlers their contribution to the development of Kenya Colony, as well as their deep sense of grievance and injustice at their treatment in a country where all the development was through their initiative. The meetings were as follows:

East Africa Indian National Congress, 1st Session, 14th March, 1914. Presidential Address by T. M. Jeevanjee in brief:

> We have not neglected our duty as loyal, industrious, enterprising, law abiding subjects of the British Crown. Winston Churchill's evidence to the Sanderson Committee of 1910 paid us a compliment. We are first and foremost businessmen not philanthropists. Business demands courage, enterprise, self-denial, strength of character, energy, capital.
> Racial prejudice in the Legislature between European settlers and Indian settlers portends future trouble.

East Africa Indian National Congress 3rd Session, 1920. President, Mr. A. M. Jeevanjee in his speech said,

> Indian industry, enterprise and labour have built up the prosperity and made East Africa such a sought after colony. Indians have borne the greater share in the military protection of the land. Indians discovered East Africa traded with it and settled there long before England discovered and traded with India. Indians possess the bulk of the trade and wealth of the land, which we have shared with the European settlers. The audacity of the European to take advantage of the foundations we have laid. He [European] has come he says to be the trustee of the black races, whom they have dispossessed of their land. Could this be true? Indian 'guardianship' has been profitable and lucrative.

Speaking of the Immigration Bill Mr. A. M. Jeevanjee said,

> I hate the so-called patience of the Asiatic races . . . you must not brook for one instant the ghost of a suggestion of inferiority. Brave, adventurous merchants came to these shores

> bearing precious gifts, the hallmark of civilization, wheat and rice which fed the body [also sugarcane and cotton which created wealth]. Gujerati speaking people from the Bombay Presidency, from Goa and all parts of the coast, you are the people who started history . . . you are the true guardians of the African interests for you did not come to colonize and exploit, but to trade.

East Africa Indian National Congress, 16th & 17th September, 1923. Mr. Hakisingh, Chairman of the Reception Committee.

Presentation of the Annual Report, starting September 1922 on 'The Indian Question'. The new Governor Sir R. Coryndon was invited to listen to the protests of the Indian community against unreasonable taxation on Indian traders.

> Poll Tax: Indians were a large community paying large sums in Poll Tax, yet the Europeans constituted a majority in the Legislative Council as well as in the Municipality. Two Indians to 16 Europeans in the Municipal Council. The population in 1926 was 25,529 Indians to 12,529 Europeans. Poll tax of course was levied according to each employed person.

In connection with the the Devonshire Declaration of 1923, an Executive Committee of East African Indian Delegates, Desai, Varma, Huseinbhai and A.M. Jeevanjee representing Kenya; Yusufali Karimjee Jeevanji and Tyeb Ali representing Tanganyaka and Uganda, travelled to London to meet the Duke of Devonshire and express their dissatisfaction. The Duke rejected the Delamere White Paper (to grant Kenya self-governing status . . .) as 'iniquitous and unjust'. The Government of India also supported the delegation and issued a Communiqué in September 1923 to boycott British goods.

Governor Coryndon had impressed on the Colonial Office that in the case of an adverse decision, the European settlers would resort to rebellion. The Colonial Office was intimidated by this threat and dared not go against the white settlers. Added to this was strong representation from General Smuts, that in case of a favourable decision to the Indians there would be serious trouble in South Africa.

It was also rumored that the Indian National Congress would claim Kenya as an Indian colony till it was ready for self-government (McKay, 1963). Denials of such rumors were useless as they reflected the fears and insecurities of the European minority. Besides, white politicians exploited these fears in order to win votes. The efforts of the European settlers to oust the Indians from East Africa did not cease, they demanded prohibition of Indian immigration maintaining that it should be done in the interest of the Africans. Mr. James Gichuru, President of the Kenya African Study Union attended one of the last Sessions of the Indian National Congress. In his speech he gave a message of goodwill to the Indian community, stating that there was plenty of room for everyone in Kenya.

Lord Delamere made a speech in Nakuru declaring that if Indians wanted franchise, restrictions would be placed on Indian immigration. The result was, increased unemployment of Indians, organized boycott of Indian goods, replacement of Indians in the public service by Europeans and other foreign nationals from Europe. Ultimately Indians had to accept lower salaries if they wished to keep their jobs.

The East Africa Indian National Congress, 1927. President, Mr. Tyeb Ali's Address on Indian settlement in Kenya.

> The first British Consulate was opened in Zanzibar to 'protect the interests' of their Indian subjects who were already there long before the British had heard of Africa. Only a few years ago Indians filled with distinction important posts as heads of departments in the Zanzibar Government. At present even unimportant positions are occupied by Europeans, which entails unnecessary burdens on the taxpayer [the Indian Merchant].

Other organizations that were set up for economic reasons but had taken a political turn were Trade Unions and Chambers of Commerce.

The East African Trade Union was founded in Kenya by Makhan

Singh, a committed trade unionist who helped Fred Kubai to work on equal rights and equal pay for the Africans. The Indian Chamber of Commerce and Industry was founded by Mr. Mahamad Kassam Lakha in Kisumu in 1932, where the first session was held. Although these organizations were set up purely for economic reasons, they soon took on a political character mainly because the settler community felt threatened by whatever the Indian introduced by way of change.

The Indian Chamber of Commerce and Industry of Eastern Africa, 1st Session, Kisumu, July 1932. Mr. Mahamad Kassam Lakha's Address welcoming Delegates:

> Economic potentiality is the bedrock on which the aspirations of the country, political and social can be built, sustained and strengthened . . .

Mr. Lakha pointed out that the community's importance was economic not political.

The East Africa Indian National Congress, 13th Session, was held in Mombasa on 26th December 1934. The welcoming address was given by Mr. K.K. Pradhan, Chairman of the Reception Committee:

> Ladies and Gentlemen, We are essentially a business community. In the history of the Indian struggle in Kenya the economic side of the problems affecting the Indians received scant attention . . . the struggle was dominated by political issues. Mr. Mahamad Kassam Lakha had indicated what part the Indian should play in the economics of Kenya. According to him 'economic potentiality is the bedrock on which the aspirations of a country, political and social can be built, sustained and strengthened.'

Later the East Africa Indian National Congress (EAINC) changed its name to Kenya Indian Congress, presumably because Zanzibar had its own Indian National Association (The first purely political association, the

National Association, had been formed in Zanzibar as early as 1920) and Uganda had the Central Council of Indian Associations.

The problem of money between Indian settlers and European settlers started in 1913 before which Kenya received an annual grant from the British Government to defray administrative expenses. After the 1914-1918 War, the Imperial Government was itself heavily indebted and could no longer support the uncontrolled settlement of approximately 200 Europeans. In addition to this, the Imperial Government had also financed the railway. However sugar produced in Muhroni from sugarcane grown on Indian plantations along with cotton grown in Kibos for export, again by Indians, had repaid the loan on the expensive railway.

In 1930 the Indian community faced a grave economic situation in all three East African territories arising from the proposal of the Government to take over the marketing of native produce in Kenya, Tanganyika and Uganda. In Zanzibar too in the clove industry, Indians faced a serious situation as a result of the enactment of various legislation aimed at destroying the economic existence of Indians whose settlement on the island dated back centuries.

The Government of India dispatched one of their most trusted persons, Mr. K.P.S. Menon, I.C.S. to inquire into the difficulties in Zanzibar and later in Kenya, Uganda and Tanganyika.

The general conclusion of the Reception Committee addressed by Mr. K.K. Pradhan was that white settlement was not self-supporting and that it was only made possible by a considerable amount of direct and indirect financial assistance. Hence the increase in tariff which was one sided -- only affecting the Indians.

Mr. K.P.S. Menon who had been sent to Zanzibar by the Indian Government to settle disputes there remarked, 'It will hardly be denied that the present policy as regards white settlement is responsible for our troubles'. Menon recommended that posts of junior personnel in Government should be filled by British Indian subjects to save money on salaries. But this proposal was not accepted and these posts continued to be held by unproductive European youths at a salary of over £500 per year.

In 1929 Isher Dass accompanied Johnston Kamau (later name Jomo Kenyatta) to London to present a Kikuyu Central Association (KCA) petition on grievances to the Colonial Office, and through his connections Mr. Dass arranged a number of public speaking engagements for Mr.

Kamau. On the land question Mr. Dass was very outspoken with the Carter Commission. He predicted future trouble between Africans and Europeans 'if a healthy and prosperous African peasantry is not created'. In 1934 Dass presented petitions by the Maasai, the KCA and the Progressive Kikuyu Party, to the Legislative Council. In 1938 he got involved in a Kamba protest march which led to the arrest of Samuel Muindi Mbingu. In fact Mr. Dass spent most of his political life in the Legislative Council promoting appeals for African representation in the Legislature. Apparently his deeds were not well taken, he was accused of incitement and assassinated in 1942.

In 1931 A.B Patel and V.V. Phadke stated to the Colonial Government their whole-hearted support for His Majesty's Government's pledge to the African people of 'trusteeship that cannot be devolved'.

'If it were not for the Indian politicians, Kenya would have long ago become a white colony like South Africa and Rhodesia.' -- (Masinde Muliro, 1960).

Chapter 8

Indians and the British

The charm that the Indian has for trade is comparable only to that the European has for colonizing.
(Sir Bartle Frere)

The first visit of a British ship to Zanzibar was that of the East Indiaman's *Edward Bonaventure* on 7, November 1591 in the reign of Queen Elizabeth I, under the command of Sir James Lancaster. It remained in port till 15, February 1592 much to the chagrin of the Portuguese whose permission they had not taken. The words of Queen Elizabeth giving her blessing to the English company were well remembered. The promoters were to:

> . . . adventure after merchandise, gold, pearl, jewels and other commodities which are to be bought, bartered, procured, exchanged or otherwise obtained (Hall, 1996).

Next to visit East Africa were the *Orestes* and *Leopard* in 1799 on their way to India. In fact Britain had not the slightest interest in East Africa at this time.

British presence in India was very different from their presence in any of their other colonies. They went to the court of the Moghul Emperor as suppliants for trade. The Moghul Empire was a powerful one based on a civilization that had used writing for more than 2,000 years at the time. In India there were no white settlers who intended to stay, as in Africa. During the last thirty years of British rule in India officials in the highest service were Indian. Nevertheless Britain had been in India for 400 years by then. Unfortunately the Moghul Empire being in a state of flux at the time of their arrival, the conquest of India by the British through trickery was made easy. The political change began in 1757 and was completed by 1857.

The British Empire established control over the peoples of India and annexed large territories of Asia and Africa as well. Britain played the main role in the expansion of Europe, wars fought in Europe were settled in the colonies. If France lost a war with Britain in Europe, Britain acquired overseas territories of the French as in the case of Mauritius and Seychelles. Germany contributed Tanganyika in East Africa to the British Empire after they lost the 1914-1918 World War.

The process of British conquest of India had its own economic rationale. India was occupied and brought under firm control during the years 1760-1858, coinciding with the 1760-1840 Industrial Revolution pioneered in England. Unlike North America, British India was not merely a settlement to displace the natives and settle on their land. The British meant to rule India and exploit the toil of the Indian peasantry in the production of cheap raw materials for the benefit of an industrial Britain.

From the early 17th century onwards colonization and trade were inseparable, and shipping was closely tied to both (Condiff, 1951). For many centuries Indians had been established along the East African coastal region and whether under Arab or Portuguese rule the Indian community particularly had prospered. So far the British had only considered the East African coast as a re-stocking and transit station, never as a lucrative trading or settlement post. However when the British found so much interest taken by other western nations they felt compelled to investigate the activities of their Indian subjects in East Africa.

As far as anyone knows Capt. Thomas Smee's visit to Zanzibar in 1811 as a Bombay Government representative, was the first time an agent of the British authorities in India had taken any interest in the operations of their British Indian subjects in East Africa. Ever since Capt. Smee and Lt. Hardy reported that the wealthy Hindu traders had 'engrossed the greatest part of the trade' the British had been planning to capture this trade for themselves. The British Government resolved that so long as this trade served British interests and British goods, to initiate a cash economy, Indian trading would be sanctioned and protected. That would be the privilege of the Indian as British subjects.

The Indian merchant class was the dominant group in this trade network. British imperialism took root with the realization that their subjects controlled the East African markets and that the great potential of these markets could only be tapped with the cooperation of these Indian merchants - and their capital. Of crucial importance to the British were the well consolidated agencies of the Indian merchants. It was only through these agencies that British manufactured goods could be distributed to the entire East African region. With their maritime experience, and knowledge of the various media of exchange, they were very important to British designs. The British also knew that they could count on Indian merchant cooperation for two reasons; firstly because they were British Indian subjects and secondly because many of these merchants were agents of established British firms in India. In essence through these firms they were already exporting British commodities to Europe and America in the form of British iron - iron ore imported into India from East Africa by the Indians, consequently Indian products became British. Also, British textiles were imported into India from Britain, they then made their way to East Africa through British Indian merchants and exporters.

The British made Bombay, which had become the storehouse for East African, Arabian and Persian commerce, the seat from which they aimed to control the Indian Ocean trade. In 1820 the policy of granting political support and privileges to Indian merchants in Zanzibar as British subjects engaged in 'legitimate trade' (as opposed to the slave trade) began to show imperialist aims. After the abolition of slavery, Indian merchants lent money to Arabs to hire labour for their plantations. Through defaulting in loan repayment the Indian ended up owning the plantation. However the British had no desire to see Arabs ousted from the clove plantations. They preferred that the Indians confine themselves to trading and selling and the Arabs continue to own the clove plantations. Hence they introduced Decrees (see Chapter 5) which disadvantaged the Indians and favoured the ruling class, the Arabs. The trading firms of other imperialist nations in Europe and North America were allowed to carry on trading with Indians in East Africa as long as they did not threaten British interests.

From1824-1826 Britain had followed a policy of political support for Indian merchants trading with the Sultan's possessions in Mombasa. Under the circumstances the influence of the British Government in India over the Sultan of Zanzibar increased.

The second contact made by the British with East Africa was when two British ships sailed to Africa and Asia, 1821-1826, under the command of

Capt. F.W. Owen. He recorded contact with Indians during his East African stay, but his main interest was in the Sultan of Zanzibar's possessions on the Mombasa coast and the Mazruis' 'offer' of Mombasa to the British in exchange for protection.

At this stage British interest was actually concentrated on the activities of Indian merchants in Zanzibar and not in the port of Mombasa or the Mazruis' problems with the Sultan of Zanzibar (See Chapter 4 for Mombasa and the Mazruis).Capt. Atkins Hamerton of the Indian army was appointed Her Majesty's Consul in 1841 to make sure that the activities of the Indians worked in Britain's favour.

THE FIRST BRITISH CONSUL IN ZANZIBAR

An extract from *Chronicles of the Indian Societies in Zanzibar* by Hindu Sheth states:

> It is interesting as to how the British Government first arranged to have a British Consul at the Zanzibar Sultan's court under the pretext of safeguarding the interests of the large number of British Indians [residing in Zanzibar]. This 'solicitude' on the part of the British Government to safeguard Indian interests was ludicrous, but politics has always been a crooked game.
>
> The then Governor General of India wrote to the Sultan of Zanzibar of the wish to have a Consul to safeguard the interests of the large number of British Indian subjects. The Sultan saw no necessity for that and the Indians themselves did not want a Consul, being happy and contented under the Sultan's rule. But the Imperial Government would not allow this rebuff to its policy. So some prominent British officers in the employment of the Sultan approached prominent Indians not to raise objections to the appointment of a British Consul. Being unsophisticated and interested in their businesses they agreed, so the Sultan gave his consent.

Capt. Atkins Hamerton's first encounter with Seyyid Said as British Consul was over British Indians, and whose subjects they were for the purposes of taxes. He maintained that the hundreds of Indians residing in Zanzibar and along the coast were British subjects and would always have the Queen's protection. Soon after Hamerton was appointed Consul, Jairam Sewji attempted to persuade the local Indians to sign a declaration repudiating their status as British subjects and declaring themselves subjects of the Sultan. Many of them refused and even preferred to leave Zanzibar, as the Indians did require British protection from time to time. Hamerton remarked, 'The banyans leaving the place would at once ruin the revenue.' So no more was heard about the change of allegiance. They remained independent yet protected.

Hamerton's successor General Christopher Rigby again attempted to repeat 'British protection' of Indian merchants. Since most of them originated from the British protected State of Cutch they did not consider themselves British subjects. Eventually the Rao (ruler) of Cutch was persuaded by the Bombay Government to issue a Proclamation whereby his subjects residing in Zanzibar were brought under the protection of the British Consul.

A judicial system as well, was established for British Indians. From 1861 the British Consular Court established at Zanzibar by virtue of the earlier Treaties of 1822 and 1839, gave them jurisdiction over British subjects with an appeal to the High Court of Bombay. In 1890 Her Britannic Majesty's High Court was established in Zanzibar. Most of the British subjects, numbering 5,000 on the mainland and 6,000 in Zanzibar over whom it had jurisdiction in 1863, were Indian.

In the early years of European trade in Zanzibar British trade in East Africa was insignificant compared with that of America, France and Germany, although the activities of Indian traders was significant enough to warrant the appointment of a British Consul from 1841 onwards. After the accession of Seyyid Bargash in 1871 Sir John Kirk was appointed Consul-General at Zanzibar, paid by the Bombay Government and directly responsible to them.

During most of the 19th century the growth of British influence in Zanzibar was closely linked with Indian trade. Sir John Kirk remarked, 'It is entirely through the Indian merchants that we were enabled to build up influence that resulted in our position' in East Africa. Indian mercantile influence continued but it was bound to and influenced by Britain's industrial needs. Actually by way of trade Britain had virtually nothing to offer, such trade as existed between India and Zanzibar consisted wholly of Indian goods. As Indian trade increased so did British influence in Zanzibar.

Equally important to British trade was the improvement in communications, which resulted in the establishment of a steamer between Bombay and Zanzibar. In 1872 a group of businessmen, retired consular officials and philanthropists led by a Scottish shipping magnate Sir William Mackinnon, founded the British Indian Steam Navigation Company (B.I.S.N.Co.) and formed themselves into the British East Africa Association. In 1887, the Association in an agreement with the Sultan of Zanzibar, obtained political rights to the stretch of coast north and south of Mombasa in return for an annual fee equal to the amount previously received in custom duties. In 1888 the Association was granted a Royal Charter and became the Imperial British East Africa Company (I.B.E.A.C.).

Gradually Seyyid Said was becoming a puppet of the British *raj*. The Zanzibar Arabs were afraid of what would happen in view of Britain's 'grasping policy' in India. Lord Dalhousie had even sent Queen Victoria the famous Koh-i-Noor diamond the symbol of Sikh nationalism, as a present (Hall, 1996). British steam power was conquering the Monsoons. British ships were no longer dependent on the wind pattern, consequently the Indian dhow became obsolete. As a result Indian ship owners were put out of business.

Chapter 9

Indians and Arabs

The importance of the relationship between these two peoples cannot be over emphasized for it pre-dates the history of their contact with Africa. Indians and Arabs were the first to discover the importance of the Monsoon winds to facilitate their trading activities in the Indian Ocean. In fact both nations acknowledged that trade was the key to prosperity and progress. Even though the Arabs had virtually nothing to trade they were indeed sailors and traders. Their first trading outpost was the Bay of Cambay on the west coast of India from where they obtained their trading goods. Trading between these two nations may have taken place before written records existed.

The Arabs were not the only adventurers on the African coast, for the Trade Winds which proved so useful to them also carried Indian traders to the East African coast and provided them with the same regular return journey. Indians had no need to consider settling in other countries unlike the Arabs who spread out as rulers all along the coast of Arabia and eventually East Africa, where they found fertile land. Although some Indians did have trading posts and personnel in East Africa, they thought of themselves as traders and were quite content to engage in commerce while always considering India as their home. Indian traders did not at first establish settlements of their own but later there were frequent references to *banyans* in Zanzibar and Mombasa. It seems that Indians were content to trade under the protection of Arabs after the latter had recovered possession of their settlements in East Africa. Therefore peaceful trade and co-existence prevailed.

Arab merchants from Yemen and their Hindu counterparts from Gujerat traded around the markets of southern Arabia. Arab trade consisted of aromatic gums from Hadhramaut (Ancient southern Arabian kingdom that occupied South East Yemen and present day Sultanate of

Oman), and frankincense and myrrh from Somalia in exchange for cinnamon, renowned Indian swords, glass, cloth, brass, silver plate, small axes, adzes, clarified butter (ghee) and wheat from India. Hadhramaut maintained its independence until AD 3 when it was conquered by the Kingdom of Saba or Sabea (now Aden).

The long distance trade was in the hands of Indians and Arabs but the Africans controlled access to the products of their own country. The Hindu merchants carried to India, ivory, rhinoceros horn, tortoise shell and gold from Zimbabwe. Ivory had been an important export as early as the 2nd century BC. Ivory was important in Islamic culture for a time but the demand declined. Not so however the Indian demand which on the contrary increased. Indians preferred the soft African ivory to the hard Indian product which was difficult to carve into bangles for Hindu brides.

Indian traders from Cutch, Porbander and Surat had been traditionally in Muscat for a very long time. They had sailed to Oman, set up trade and worked in various capacities. Their ability for business had won the confidence of the Imams as financiers and customs collectors. But Indians were valued in Arab countries above all for their bookkeeping and accounting abilities. They were astute businessmen and good managers of the Sultan's wealth. They also provided technical and such services as the Arabs were unable or reluctant to engage in.

The first Arab settlements on the East African coast date from about AD 800. By the 12th century Arab settlement dominated a great part of the 'Zanj' coast in the nature of an Arab empire, even though the Imam ruled from Muscat. At first the Arabs were resentful of Indian presence and allowed them to stay only at the Swahili coast and for just one season of the Monsoons. They feared the commercial competition but tolerated them because they were dependent on their capital. Indian involvement in Arab trading expeditions was by supplying funds, equipment and trade goods. Zanzibar under the Imam of Muscat was administered by a *Hakim* or Governor, a slave of the Imam's who demanded unreasonable taxes from the Indian merchants.

When the Arabs moved to the East African coast to establish residence there, the Indians were persuaded to accompany them purely as financial advisers. However the first Indian trade settlements were in Zanzibar and in spite of the apparent friendship between Arabs and Indians, the Arabs did not hesitate to loot Indian dhows whenever the opportunity presented itself.

During Capt. F.W. Owen's voyage to Africa and Arabia (1821-1826) he recorded commercial relations in East Africa between Arabs and Indians. He gave an account of conditions of Indian traders in Mombasa. The Indian merchant was helpless and unprotected and had to submit to the swindles of the Arab who wished to procure goods on credit but did not wish to pay for them. An American naval officer calling at Zanzibar in 1835 observed that the *banyans* were despised by the Arabs because of their avarice and thrift and also because they submitted to insults and indignity. Burton the explorer described the Indian as 'right meek beside the Arab fierceness' and that they rose in mercantile repute by qualities of commercial integrity. 'They rarely indulge in a siesta unless rich enough to afford such a luxury'. While contemporary observers made adverse remarks about Indians they also emphasized their frugality, industriousness and perserverance.

Indians had been trading on the coast of East Africa from very ancient times. Originally they were 'obliged to make Zanzibar via Maskat in a certain ship'. From the 10th to the 18th centuries this coastal trade was mainly in the hands of Arab and Indian dhow traders. But Indian influence on the East African coast was substantially increased by the 19th century as Arabs did not possess much business acumen or inclination towards hard work. Much of the Indian Ocean shipping was Indian owned and Indian manned.

According to Sir R. Coupland:

> Much of the trade is Indian owned and Indian manned since Arabs in general seem never to have shown much aptitude for the technique of business.

The actual trade was either in Indian hands or managed by them for the wealthy land-owning Arab proprietors. The Indians monopolized the lesser retail trade and the Arabs had to pay in the long term for not taking an interest in it themselves. For, dependence on Indian industry and skill made the Arabs rich but weakened their economic independence and initiative.

The Arabs of Africa were 'an aristocracy of race'. Closely associated with them but not of the ruling class were the Indian residents whose connection with the East African coast was as old as theirs if not older.

There were no Hindu converts to Islam in Africa, the community kept their religious beliefs, customs and language.

Arabs and Hindus were natural enemies but by diplomacy Seyyid Said was able to combine their assets; the financial acumen of the banyan with the toughness of the Arab soldier and trader, to the advantage of all. Seyyid Said forged an alliance between Arab and Indian businessmen. He planted extensive clove plantations on Zanzibar and Pemba islands, owned by Arabs and backed by Indian capital. East Africa gained its place in the network of trade from the 'Zanj' coast through Arab and Indian efforts. In spite of Arab aggression, Indians lived in complete harmony with the Arabs and Africans.

The Moghuls came to trade with India from the north of the sub-continent in about AD 636. At first they were well received, they even married Hindu women who converted to Islam. But this relationship took a new turn with the conquest of northern India by the Moghuls. By the 13th century Muslims became the masters of Delhi. From 1392 Gujerat on the west coast became a Muslim kingdom. From the 16th century onwards Islam began to cross the Indus. Slavery was always practiced by the Arabs but after their influence in India increased, slavery took on vast proportions. Muslim rulers kept slaves, both men and women to serve them.

In about AD 916 also, merchants of Hormuz in South Arabia settled as a trading community on the Malabar coast in southwest India, where they established friendly relations with the Zamorin or Sea King (a hereditary title) of Calicut. Some of the Indian States located on the western coast, the Malabar and Rastakuta Kingdoms were friendly towards Muslims and permitted Arab traders to trade and even settle in Daibul and Cambay.

Chapter 10

Indians and Portuguese

> **Where India lay was but a hazy notion, at this time India included Southern Arabia, Ethiopia, East Africa and even the East Indies. It would be more accurate to say that India was those lands whence came the costly products such as spices, aromatics and precious stones that were necessary for the comfort and adornment of the powerful and wealthy in Europe.**
> (Justus Strandes In *The Portuguese Period in East Africa,* 1989)

Special attention should be given to Portuguese settlement in East Africa since it is a fallacy to believe that the Portuguese 'opened up' Africa as stated in Sir Harry Johnston's book *The Opening up of Africa.* It is also an error to state that the Portuguese were the first foreigners to discover East Africa and to bring 'civilization and goods' with them.

> Indian dhows brought spices and other luxury goods up the Red Sea 'in large ships where the Muslims (Egyptians) go to purchase them, they loaded them on camels and other beasts of burden for the markets of Cairo and other places on the Mediterranean'. In those markets the buyers of pepper and silk and other oriental products, were merchants from Italy, chiefly from Genoa and Venice. This was the trade that the Portuguese longed to usurp.

India is not only 'those lands whence came the costly products . . .

necessary for the adornment of the powerful and wealthy in Europe'. In 1920 A.M. Jeevanjee, addressing the East Africa Indian National Congress said:

> . . . Brave adventurous merchants came to these shores [East Africa] bringing precious gifts, the hallmark of civilization, wheat, rice . . .

The Portuguese were obsessed with finding a sea route to the spice producing countries and they had a fair idea that following the African coastline would do that. Throughout the 15th century the Portuguese had been slowly feeling their way down the west coast of Africa. From the beginning of 1487 voyages were undertaken, each time going further down the west African coast putting up pillars to reassure themselves of the safety thus far. They also had to reassure superstitious sailors who were afraid to sail too far for fear of 'falling off the face of the earth', until on 8th July 1497 after seventy years of trial they were finally ready to venture out of European waters, in four ships.

When Vasco da Gama arrived at the much feared Cape of Good Hope on 27, November 1497 his crew was near mutiny and wished to go no further. For several weeks the ships had to struggle with stormy seas; they did not realize that the worst was over. The fleet rounded the Cape of Good Hope on 25, December 1497 and sighted the coast of Natal, named by the Portuguese for Christmas day. At Natal they took in fresh water and food. They made one more stop where two sailors were left with one ship to explore and search for Prester John, the fabled priest-king of the east, the most persistent fantasy of the middle ages. Prester John was supposedly reigning in Ethiopia and helping to vanquish the infidels - the Muslims. However if the Portuguese who disembarked at the Cape were hoping to meet up with him they had a long walk ahead of them.

From Sofala on the east coast the Portuguese in their three ships passed one agreeable surprise after another, gone were the gray months on the Atlantic. They came upon busy ports and populous coastal cities. They met sailors who knew the seaways to India and beyond, who sailed with charts and compasses, with knowledge of the world wider than their own. They watched a flourishing maritime trade, a world of commerce larger and wealthier than Europe knew. They were surprised at the ease and substance of the ports that they sheltered in and plundered. They in turn were disregarded as uncouth and strange.

In February 1498 when Vasco da Gama's flotilla of three ships anchored off the coast of Mozambique, his logbook records that he 'found the country in the possession of Arabs and Indians whose self-interest was in getting rich'. The population according to him was 6,000 negro slaves and a garrison of 200, chiefly Arabs and Indians. The Arab settlements were known as the 'Zenj' empire.

The first important people that Vasco da Gama met were the Sheikh of Mozambique and his retinue. They were dressed in robes of velvet and silk with gold thread. Their turbans were of silk and gold, they carried swords and daggers of mounted silver. As stated earlier, among the Arab settlements the state of Kilwa took the lead. At Kilwa Vasco da Gama was given two pilots to guide him to India but when it was discovered that they were Gujerati Hindus and not Christians as they claimed, the Portuguese became hostile towards them.

On 7, April 1498 the three Portuguese ships sailed up the Mozambique channel and anchored off the coast of Mombasa, but they were not at all well received so they sailed north to Malindi.

An unknown chronicler writes:

> That same day at sunset we cast off anchor at a place called Milinde, which is thirty leagues from Mombaza.

The Sultan of Malindi received them well. At Malindi the guides were replaced by two new pilots to guide the Portuguese to India. One Mallim Kanaka, a Gujerati who claimed to have converted to Christianity and the other, Ahmad ibn Majid, a Muslim introduced as 'the Moor of Gujerat'.

Of the two guides it is Ahmad ibn Majid who draws the greater attention. In 1422 Ahmad ibn Majid of various names, was identified by Gabriel Fernand as the greatest Arab pilot of the 15th century. A very cultured man, a native of Djulfar in Oman. A pilot of that time had multiple responsibilities. Next in importance to the owner of the ship the pilot was responsible for the safety of the crew, merchandise and state of the ship; he had to have nautical, practical and scientific knowledge. Majid had dedicated his life to seafaring from Guardafui to Sofala on the East African coast, India, Malaya and China. He shared his knowledge by writing four 'rutters' (Correa-Alfonse, 1964). He was a very remarkable source of nautical information in Arabic. The material in other oriental languages is scarce but there exists some in Persian and some Indian languages.

On 24, April 1498 the Portuguese set sail for India with Ahmad ibn Majid who came on board with charts and his own nautical instruments. He was knowledgeable, cheerful and confidant, the Portuguese could not have got a better guide. They called him Malena Canaque, Captain Astrologer, as a tribute to his skill in reading the stars. They left Malindi on 24, April and in three weeks ibn Majid took the Portuguese safely to India, though he cursed himself later for agreeing to do so. The Portuguese plundered and looted the rich Indian Ocean countries they stopped at, they battered down cities and sailed away with the loot.

On 18, May 1498 land was sighted and they anchored at Calicut off the west coast of India. Da Gama prepared to meet the most powerful ruler on the Indian coast, the Rajah of Calicut, the 'pepper port'. He had letters of introduction from King Manuel of Portugal. The Rajah of Calicut, Mana Vikram, the Zamorin, was a Hindu with Buddhist leanings. His principals were free trade and respect for foreign shipping, consequently Vasco da Gama was well received.

At Calicut the Portuguese loaded up with spices, pepper and ginger. The Zamorin, The Sea King, treated them well and they set off in 1499 on their return journey. The voyage which had taken three weeks eastwards now took three months. It was 'plagued with contrary winds' and they did not have their 'Malindi pilot' with them. Ahmad ibn Majid had deserted them as soon as they landed in India. He had regretted offering to guide the Portuguese in the first instance and news of their looting preceded them, so that merchants hid their wares. Thereafter the Portuguese continued to make yearly visits to India.

For as long as they could the Portuguese tried to keep the secret of the East from all seekers of fabrics, spices and porcelain. It was an offence for any Portuguese to sell a map, sea-charts of the Indian Ocean or any information on the Estado da India. The Portuguese now dominated the spice trade with India. The new route to India via the Cape although longer than through Egypt and the Red Sea, was more economical since much money was saved by not having to pay taxes and bribes.

On leaving India Vasco da Gama had extracted a promise from the Rajah of Calicut that when the spice auctions commenced the next year they would be given precedence over the powerful and long established Arab merchants living in the city. So when the time came for the auctions

Map: East African coast before 1600
Source: History of Africa by Kevin Shillington, pg. 126

trouble broke out between the Arabs and the Portuguese. Arab ships were captured and fifty three Portuguese were killed. This trip was made under the command of Captain Cabral.

On Vasco da Gama's second voyage to India in 1502 he punished the city of Calicut for the death of his fifty three compatriots. All Arab ships lying in the harbour were bombarded and set ablaze, those who managed to escape by jumping into the sea were shot down with arrows, not even the people on the shore were allowed to help survivors. Mana Vikran, Rajah of Calicut had to flee his palace, a humiliation he would never live down. The Portuguese now dominated the European spice trade.

The 'Island of Goa' (Goa is not an island, it is an integral part of the Indian sub-continent) was captured and Alfonse d'Albuquerque was appointed the first Governor. Goa lived up to Albuquerque's expectations of becoming a prosperous enclave with reminders of life in Europe. The natural harbour was most suited to Portuguese activities who established their trade at the expense of Indian and Arab trade, the monopoly of which had been secured by a Papal Bull.

An anonymous Portuguese navigator wrote of India's contact with East Africa long before the 15th century. There was also the Portuguese official Duarte Barbosa who retired to Indonesia, having served Vasco da Gama in India between 1500 and 1516. He left accounts of the commercial trade carried on between Cambay, a sea port in Gujerat, and Africa. Cambay is actually an inlet of the Arabian Sea on the west coast of India between Kathiawar and the Gujerati coast. Cambay was later supplanted by Bombay due to silting. Barbosa records trade between Indians and the coast south of Zanzibar:

> Indians came in small *zambucos* [the Portuguese name for the small sailing boats] bringing cotton cloth, *kambaye* -- white and indigo dyed from Cambay, silks, small beads (grey, yellow and red) which came from the kingdom of Cambay in other greater ships up to Zanzibar. And these wares the Moors who came from Malindi and Mombasa purchased from others who bring hither and pay in gold as merchants depart well pleased.

Kilwa had become the central trading station for gold brought down from Sofala, the center of the gold supply which came from inland, mainly from Zimbabwe. Indians came with Indian goods in *jahazis* to exchange for gold and ivory.

> The Moors kept these wares and sold them later to the heathen king of Benepeta. They collect great stores of ivory which they find hard by Sofala and also this they sell to the Kingdom of Cambay. These Moors are black and some are tawny.

The town of Kilwa was taken by the Portuguese 'as moved by arrogance the Sharif refused to obey the Portuguese King and Lord'. The Sharif was forced to acknowledge the supremacy of the King of Portugal and pay tribute in gold. The population at this important trading post dwindled so much that its historical importance ended.

On their first voyage the Portuguese had somehow missed Sofala, but on their second visit they occupied the town. The occupation of Sofala, Barbosa says was no trouble. The Sultan offered no resistance and paid the required tribute to the King of Portugal.

The Portuguese then proceeded to Mombasa which had shown them so much hostility on their first visit in 1498. Mombasa had dominated the coastal trade in the 12th century. The people were black, white and tawny. There were signs of affluence everywhere, the women wore gold ornaments, there were lofty houses of stone and mortar having carved wooden doors 'with excellent joinery'. Ships came from the 'Kingdom of Cambay' bringing sheep with round tails, cows and fowls, much millet, rice, sweet and bitter oranges, lemons, pomegranates, Indian figs and vegetables. The men from the hinterland (Nyika tribe) were often at war with the inhabitants of Mombasa, nevertheless they still brought their wares such as wax, honey and ivory, to the coast to trade.

The Portuguese sent an envoy to the ruler of Mombasa offering friendship and protection if his 'country' became subjects of the Portuguese crown. This offer was met with resistance from 1,500 bowmen from the interior and the town's people. A battle was fought in the narrow streets of Mombasa and the population was driven back with much loss of life.

> The king of the city refused to obey the command of the King and Lord so through his arrogance he lost it.

The Portuguese took Mombasa by force and the Sheikh had to flee. His people were plundered of gold, silver, amber and other rich wares including carpets of unequaled beauty. They even took the cattle and provisions, so much so that 800 prisoners had to be set free for lack of space on their ships. This prosperous town was set ablaze before they departed.

There exists a letter that the Sheikh of Mombasa sent to the Sheikh of Malindi warning him about the imminent visit from the Portuguese, 'There is no living thing, all those who failed to escape were killed. Be on your guard.' But Malindi was spared because of the hospitality the Portuguese received on their first visit and because of this friendship the Sheikh was offered some of the loot and a privileged status. Barbosa described Malindi as a town with well laid out streets,

> The people were great barterers of gold and ivory. They traded with the heathen merchants from the kingdom of Cambay who make great profits from their cargoes and merchandise. The King and people were ever friends of the King of Portugal who obtained supplies in plenty from them.

The Portuguese were allowed to build a monument to commemorate their landing in Malindi.

Between the islands of Sao Lorenço (Madagascar) and the mainland are three islands, Pemba, Mafia and Zanzibar. Zanzibar known as the Green Island was the most productive of the three.

> Great stores of food, rice, fleshmeat, vegetables, oranges, limes, citrons and every kind of fruit abound. The King of these isles lives in great luxury, dressed in fine silks and cotton garments which they purchase at Mombasa from Cambay merchants.

Sugarcane was introduced into Zanzibar from India as were mangoes, jackfruit and in fact all the tropical fruit growing on the island. After some fighting the Portuguese departed on the promise of an annual tribute in gold to the King of Portugal. Lamu succumbed and paid tribute to the

Portuguese king.

Mogadishu was described as a fine Moorish town on the Red Sea. Many ships called here from the 'Kingdom of Cambay' bringing cloth and divers other wares, taking away gold, ivory, gums copal and arabic, and wax. In this town the Portuguese found wheat, barley, horses and fruit of divers kinds, a place of great wealth, but few weapons. 'They use "herbs" on their weapons to defend themselves.' This town also the Portuguese took without much ado.

The Portuguese imported beads, calico and other goods from India exchanging them for ivory, gold and eventually slaves. They went into the slave trade with such enthusiasm that 'no African was safe at the coast for even a day'.

On Vasco da Gama's second visit to East Africa in 1502, the Portuguese planned to establish supremacy over the coasts of the Indian Ocean by plunder, by demanding tribute to the Portuguese crown and by building forts at all the major ports. These Portuguese forts were to house a Portuguese garrison.

For thousands of years the old trade routes were remarkably peaceful. No empires, no human dangers, no pirates to disrupt the trade. Until in 1498 came Vasco da Gama bringing European warfare and atrocities. The earliest travellers, both who came from the north and those who came with Vasco da Gama round the Cape, found Indian traders at every port along the coast carrying on a very considerable trade between India and Africa. This peaceful trade and co-existence was sorely crippled and in parts extinguished by the arrival of Europeans to those areas. They destroyed Indian and Arab maritime life. They practiced cruelties on all those who opposed them. They were determined to seize the Indian Ocean trade for themselves and to accumulate as much personal wealth as possible by piracy and plunder. According to the Memoirs of Captain Singleton:

> Active young men went into those seas and plundered everybody, but especially the Indian merchants without any sense of wrongdoing.

At the coming of the Portuguese, Indian traders were in possession of the best trade from Sofala to Aden. The Portuguese were most powerful at sea, they subdued the whole coast from the Cape to the limit of the

Indian trade northwards to Aden. Thus in the space of a mere ten years they managed to destroy the trade and cultural life that had taken centuries to evolve. The long established control of the coasts and waters of the Indian Ocean passed into European hands. At sea they looted Arab and Indian ships as a matter of course and even on land, gold, ivory and other traditional goods from inland tribes were to be sold to the Portuguese and also bought from them. For the Arabs and Indians the result of Portuguese hegemony was devastating. Deprived of their livelihood many Indians abandoned their trade or kept it to a bare minimum.

Having wrecked the Afro-Asian trade of the Indian Ocean by exacting tribute and by piracy, the Portuguese tried to restore it to their own advantage. In this they failed and were even superceded by the Dutch. At Kilwa, the main trading post of the time, the Portuguese had taken the place of Arabs as middlemen. They imported calico and beads from India exchanging them for gold, ivory and eventually slaves. Unlike the Arabs who sent caravans into the interior to buy and sell, the Portuguese did not venture into the interior of Africa. They imagined that if they kept up a supply of Indian goods in their warehouses in Sofala the Africans would come to them with goods from the interior to exchange.

The Portuguese were less successful at trading than the Indians and so after 1804 sea piracy was rampant both among the Arabs and the Portuguese. Indian cargoes were targeted indiscriminately, however the unwarlike Hindus sought only to elude the pirates rather than fight. They sheltered in the numerous inlets on the Arabian coast till the danger was passed.

The Portuguese endeared themselves neither to Indians nor Arabs. In fact they were actually expelled from Muscat where they had built a fort in 1651-1652. Although the reason for their expulsion might seem amusing now, it was serious enough at the time to cause an international incident. Pereira, the Portuguese Commandant of the Fort, fell in love with the beautiful daughter of the chief Indian merchant in Muscat. This influenced the otherwise non-interfering Indians to seek assistance from the Arabs to attack the Portuguese garrison on a Sunday, when many of the defenders were reeling drunk.

By 1700 the Portuguese abandoned their plan to trade and settled in Mozambique to colonize. Mozambique was colonized in 1507 and like Goa, became an External Province of Portugal. The other possessions of the Portuguese were Ibo, an island about five kilometres in length, and Cape Delgado. These properties were used for the purpose of collecting dues. They also kept three ships at anchor off the coast of Mozambique. In 1545 St. Francis Xavier wrote of the Portuguese:

> Opportunities of plunder, their appetites for gain will be sharpened as they taste it. Robbery is so public and common that it hurts no one's character and is hardly counted a fault.

Chapter 11

The Indian trader

> **Hats off to the Indian dukawalla who survived through this period often on the meager profits they made by selling packing cases in which they brought their goods.**
> (Apa Bala Pant, India's 1st High Commissioner to East and Central Africa)

Indians recognized very early in their civilization the economic advantages and civilizing effects of trade. The first for offering better prospects for power and the second for introducing new products for improving the quality of life.

The Indian trader originated generally from the hot and arid regions of India. Commonly known as *banyans* and *merwars* the Indian trader came from Sindh, Cutch, Kathiawar, Surat, Calicut and other parts of the Malabar coast. He arrived in Zanzibar at an early age and was apprenticed to another Indian merchant. It was only after many years that he could revisit his native land, marry and set up business for himself, either in Africa or his home country.

From time immemorial Gujerat because of its long coastline and proximity to the commercial and cultural zones, was exposed to contact with other regions, East Africa, Middle East and South East Asia. For centuries also Gujeratis were found trading in various parts of the world. The whole traffic in those pre-steamer days was carried out in small sailing boats called *dhows* and *gurabs*. These used to come from and return to India in their 'proper seasons'.

Merchant seamen on the coastal ports of western India embarked on their voyages as soon as the 'Star of Agastya' had been sighted. Agastya, the saint who pioneered sea pilgrims in spreading a new culture among the people he encountered on his voyages. His travels took him to Cambodia, Java, Sumatra, Ceylon, Bali and Indonesia. References to Agastya and his teachings from the *Ramayana* depicted in paintings, are found in the literature of these islands. The seamen watched eagerly for their 'guiding light, the regular change' in ocean currents signifying calm seas, the homage that the ocean paid to Agastya, as described in the *Puranas*. Travellers to East Africa knew that the time had come for them to leave India.

When the time came for leave-taking the whole village assembled at the shore the night before. Some of the passengers were as young as twelve years, leaving home for the first time. The seamen performed their *puja*, the voyagers together with their families bowed to their god bringing offerings of coconuts and sweet rice. The women placed a *tilak* (red dot) on the forehead of the travelling husband, brother or son for good luck, giving him a piece of 'sugar candy' to bring him back safely. They pledged to fast and perform *puja* to the moon on the second day of each new moon. Only then would the travellers board the dhows and depart, watched by their families till they were out of sight. Leave-taking scenes were a common occurrence at many ports on the Gujerati coast at this time (Kotecha, 1994).

The minimum cost of travel was Rs 10. Those who could not afford the fare were welcome on board on the understanding that they would pay later, and they always did. The early traveller endured many hardships. Passengers slept on deck grouped by religious communities. The Hindus were vegetarian and according to their caste culture they could not eat food cooked by anyone outside their caste. On board each man sorted out his belongings, chose his 'spot' to roll out his sleeping mat and arranged special places for cooking 'according to his caste'. Life on those small ships 80 to 350 tons, 40 to 60 ft. long, was difficult. They lacked privacy and medical facilities and even during calm weather they were sure to encounter at least two frightening storms, especially at the Equator crossing. Their only solace was in religion (Gregory, 1993).

The Captain having studied the ocean currents over a time was confident of his ability to take the ship safely to its destination. By day he steered the ship by the sun and at night by the stars. He carried on board a hundred tons of cargo and enough food and water to last the first leg of the journey to Mombasa where they again stocked up with food and water. The merchandise consisted of Surat silk embroidered with gold and silver thread, spices, diamonds, precious stones, herbs, rice and ghee. Collyrium (eye lotion) from Basra and Arabian dried dates. Even first time travellers came on board with bundles containing spices and other goods to exchange for African products on arrival at their destination.

As they approached the Equator the wind became violent and whipped up high waves. When the boat began to toss, the passengers stood up and joined hands in a circle and sang verses from the holy books. This helped to calm them and make the storm more bearable. Differences in religion and caste distinctions were forgotten, even their food was cooked in the same pot. The Captain stood at the helm, fearlessly and firmly in control of his ship, he would not relax vigilance for even a minute till the danger was passed, however long that took.

The voyage of 2,500 miles to Mombasa took at least twenty-six days. From Mombasa they sailed to Zanzibar and then down the east African coast to the treacherous crossing over the Mozambican Channel to Madagascar, where the earliest Indian settlements were.

The story of the heroism of these brave men - and their women, 'who cut a new path across the Indian Ocean' is well remembered though not recorded. These brave men set out on their own initiative with no Government support or funding, with limited education, little or no resources, and with only their faith in themselves and in God. Their trade yielded 'relatively good profits' which they shared with the whole village to raise the standard of living. At the next trading season they would be joined by more adventurers who would again risk their lives for small profit (Kotecha, 1994).

The return journey to India was undertaken at the start of the southwest Monsoons beginning in April. There were always passengers returning to their homeland. All those who wished to remit money or send letters, packed them in sealed addressed bags and handed them over to the firm of Jairam Sewji. No commission was charged by the firm. The *Malam* (Indian Captain) handled these packages with great care. The voyage took from two to eight weeks depending on favourable winds.

Those new 'traders' who joined established relatives in Zanzibar, with their language and financial problems, could not hope for any but the most menial jobs with work from dawn to dusk. Tarya Topan an Ismaili from Cutch left India at the age of twelve. He did menial jobs for Ladha Damji, Sewji's agent. He was self taught and rose to own numerous enterprises. He financed several commercial ventures as well as prominent traders like Tippu Tip. He was knighted in 1875 by the British for his assistance in suppressing the slave trade.

The majority of *dukawallahs* started out with little or no capital. They took a ninety-day loan on which they paid no interest. They concentrated on maximizing profits so that all profits were ploughed back into the business, after meeting the cost of living. There was no luxurious living, it was a spartan lifestyle. The second generation of traders as in the case of the Kassim Lakhas became economically stable so that they were able to invest in the cotton ginning industry. Nevertheless in all the economic progress wrought by the Indians in the manufacturing sector, they did not receive any government support.

Record-keeping or recording history was not a practice of the early Indian traveller. Perhaps this is linked to the caste system where the trading caste not being the literate caste was unable to write. Whereas the Brahmins, the priestly caste though literate, were not allowed to travel by sea or engage in trade. However they did travel overland, hence many historical and geographical facts have been recorded in the *Puranas* or holy books of the ancient Hindus. Therefore commercial relations between Africa and India can be reliably traced to the age of the *Puranas*, 300 BC to 700 BC. The other possibility could be that Hindu record-keeping was either perfunctory or that the writing did not survive, because on the Malabar coast writing was on fragile palm leaf sheets (Hall, 1996). Shri Dhirubhai Ghalani, whose father was among the first pioneers in East Africa, settled in Djibouti. He attributes lack of record-keeping by the early Indians to preoccupation with making a living and supporting their families rather than exploring new lands.

The coastal Hindu merchants were indifferent to the cultural and religious influences of their religion, ignoring superstitons not to cross the sea. Those who engaged in trade became wealthy and powerful and even wielded influence as 'king makers'. Thus we find in the coastal society of Gujerat that caste distinctions as well as professional groupings gave way to mercantile interests. Even Brahmins were involved in trade which according to caste restrictions was the domain of the Vaisyas, an inferior caste, and in particular the *Vania* sect of the caste.

Motivation to trade came from better economic opportunities. Their main interest was to improve their social standing among their own community in India. Although the social position of the trader is not very high in Asian countries the ruling elite were dependent on them for the creation of a market economy, or creating income by imposition of taxes without the consent of the merchants. In all Asian civilizations the merchant and the banker were indispensable in converting surplus produce, be it agriculture or money, into disposable state income. The politically powerful react favourably to the influence and demands of those who are able to command large amounts of money, hence they are granted special privileges.

Some Hindu castes whose hereditary profession was trading, converted to Islam perhaps because of the advantages in Islamic countries like the Middle East and Zanzibar. One such group is the Ismailis; diligent traders, respected in all parts of Arabia and western India, who already belonged to the Hindu trading caste, but converted to Islam. However they split from the main stock of Islam early in the history of the religion. The Bohoras 'who claim the aristocratic Brahmin caste origin' (Bakari, 1999) could only have converted to Islam because of the economic advantages, like the Ismailis. Almost every province had its 'trading castes'.

In Bombay, the Parsees by their boldness and extent of operations and nature of trade, were the more classy traders. They ventured to trade with European houses of commerce. The *Marwaris* of Rajputana are found everywhere, sometimes more important than the natives of the province. *Lohanas, Vanias, Memons, Lingayats* are found in north Madras and Mysore but generally just everywhere. The traders of Punjab are largely *Khattris.* The generic term *Banians* is included in this group, they are strictly speaking a Hindu sect. Bengal trading was dominated by Brahmins and the lower castes.

The 15th century witnessed important changes in the personnel and organization of trade with the rise to prominence of the Muslim state of Gujerat from 1392, and domination by Gujerati merchants. The industrial capital of Gujerat was Ahmedabad, which produced the cotton cloth, silks and indigo dyed cloth for which there was so much demand in Africa and Europe. The heart of the Sultanate of Gujerat was the port of Cambay on the coast, *which did not belong to the Sultanate*. Not having a port of its own Gujerat was *virtually* a land-locked state but the rulers counted on trade being carried on by its people who were protected by the State, to be left alone in their enterprise by being allowed to use the port of Cambay, as long as they contributed to its revenue by paying the required port duties and tariffs.

The merchants of Gujerat included all the major trading communities of western Asia. Among the Muslims were Arabs and Turks especially at Diu, together with Persians and Egyptians and Gujerati Muslims. The most important traders however were the Gujerati Hindus and Jains and of these the most dominant were the *Vanias*. The *Vanias* belonged to the *Vaiyas* caste, the third of the four caste divisions of 'occupational specialization'. The *Vanias* were numerically greater in a Muslim state, but they were tolerated, even celebrated, because of the revenue they brought to the State.

According to Tomé Pirès,

> They are men who understand merchandise, they are so properly steeped in the sound and harmony of it . . . they are diligent quick men of trade. They do their accounts with their fingers like ours and with our very writing. Those of our people who want to be clerks and factors ought to go and learn from them, because the business of trade is a science in itself . . .

From earliest times Gujerat had been a State of conquering and settling races. India by its vulnerability from the north, its long coastlines both east and west, had been exposed to movements of peoples and to commercial contacts with other regions. Early settlers were the Aryans who came overland from the north. Then the Persians and Arabs who came to shelter at the coast, trade or conquer. 'Gujerat was the keystone of the commercial structure of the Indian Ocean'. (Lombard, D. and Aubin, J. Eds. 1988).

The *Vanias*, the dominant trading caste, were organized in a *Mahajan*, which means a group of people engaged in the same commercial activity. These merchants from Gujerat were represented by one of their own who was appointed *Shabandar*. His main task was to look after the judicial and commercial interests of his people, manage the markets and warehouses, ensure that standards were maintained, adjudicate disputes within his community and speak for his community.

In Malacca, Malayasia, where Indians conducted a lot of trade, Indian merchants had appointed their own *Shabandar* to look after their community's interests with the ruler. The chief concentration of trade outside of Gujerat was in Malacca where about four or five thousand seamen lived at the end of the 15th century. Tomé Pirès notes that Gujerati traders were followed to Malacca by 'those of other nations'. Among these were people from Ormuz, Kilwa, Malindi, Mogadishu and Mombasa and others. Most of the traders came from the east, India, China, Indonesia, Persia, Ceylon and Arabia.

The *Shahbandar* of the Gujerati merchants was the most senior among four such officials who represented each of the foreign trading communities at Malacca. The three other *Shahbandars* represented different communities in the rest of the Indian, East Asian and East African merchants in Malacca. The activities of the Gujerati Shahbandar quite possibly were tied to these merchants through their trade in Aden.

In the Middle East they traded in various commodities, gold, saffron, vermilion and rosewater. To 'Jidda' (Jeddah) went spices, drugs and textiles from Gujerat. Trade with Aden consisted mainly of muslins from Gujerat; to Ormuz went cloves, ginger, sandalwood, brazilwood and cotton cloth; to Sofala in East Africa, cotton cloth, silk, other textiles and spices were carried inland in exchange for gold, ivory and iron ore; to Malindi and Mombasa, cotton cloth, silks and spices. Cotton cloth from India was the most important trade item.

An example of how important trade and traders are to India, is that in 1744 the Governor of the Moghul port of Surat requested the English to respect the neutrality of the port in spite of the war between England and France, 'For a city which lived by trade could not afford conflict.'

Trade with other countries including Africa and Europe made the Indians not only rich but well known world figures. Those from humble beginnings rose to positions of prominence in their countries of origin. The extensive Indian coastline both east and west, safe harbours and Monsoon winds facilitated development of maritime activity. It is believable that Indian ships with their brave sailors from the west coast of India came visiting the east coast of Africa long before recorded history. All these factors aided the Indian propensity towards trade and commercial advancement (Samson, 1993).

There is some debate on whether Arabs or Indians were the first to travel by sea to East Africa. Boat-building was an important industry in India for centuries. In keeping with the caste culture and its watertight professional divisions, the art was practiced by a section of a caste called *Badalas*. The *Badalas* were a coastal people whose traditional profession of boat-building was passed on through generations. The *Badalas* had been visiting the East African coast in their *dhows* for thousands of years and it would not be surprising if it was they who discovered the regular Monsoon winds.

When Marco Polo was travelling in India in 1270 he described the Indian merchants as 'scrupulously honest in their trading'. Goods could be left with them in complete safety by ships that came to Malabar from many parts of Asia. The Rajah of Calicut was one example. Whenever a ship was wrecked at any of his country's ports he ordered the cargo to be guarded carefully and returned to the owner.

The people of the State of Calicut were termed honest, trustworthy and distinguished. Trade was conducted in a rather unique way between representatives of the Chinese 'treasure ships' and local merchants. Chinese goods, silks, porcelain and other goods were brought ashore. Trading was a very slow process which could take up to a month or more, but eventually all parties showed their satisfaction with the deal by clasping hands. The clasping of hands showed the importance attached to trade. The Chinese were fascinated by the Indian method of calculation.

> They did not use the abacus, they use their fingers and toes and the twenty digits on them and they never make the slightest mistake (Hall, 1996).

Burton explained that the Indian trader 'rose in mercantile repute by qualities of commercial integrity'.

> They accustom their children at an early age to shun slothfulness and instead of letting them lose their time at play . . . teach them arithmetic which they learn perfectly, using for it neither pen nor counters but the memory alone. They are always with their fathers who instruct them in trade and do nothing without explaining it to them at the same time. The son is engaged in the father's trade to maintain the profession for posterity . . . Upon this account all marriages are restricted to one sect and contracted only between persons of the same persuasion and profession (Alpers, 1976).

Indian merchants had a high reputation for honesty. The wealthy

Indian firms were held in such high esteem that their 'cheques', mere pieces of paper with IOU, were honoured in Muscat, Basra and in countries west of the Suez (Kotecha, 1994) and of course all over India.

> Because Indians worked hard, lived parsimoniously and saved their earnings they were able to go into trade. The older generation settled for a low standard of living for the sake of future generations. The vast majority came to look upon Africa as their home and despite discrimination they did what they could to maintain what they felt was their rightful place (Herskovits,1958).

Chapter 12

Indians and other traders

> **As the Europeans became wealthier they came to believe that they had always enjoyed a higher civilization than Indians and Africans. They forgot that the civilization of India could not be effaced, their monuments too many, their prestige too great. The Indian trade might be ruined but their greatness survived.**
> (Basil Davidson in *Old Africa Rediscovered*, 1958)

For all the importance of local trade it was international trade that created the wealth that brought Eastern Africa to the sphere of the world economy. The traders that came from India and Arabia would meet Chinese and Indonesians but no Europeans are known to have come to Africa before the 15th century. At the end of the 15th century all that changed. Europeans opened the route that gave them direct access by sea to the East and placed Africa in their path (Newitt, 1995).

For as long as they could the Portuguese tried to keep the secret of the route to India via the Cape from seekers of spices, fabrics and porcelain. However within twenty-five years of Vasco da Gama's voyage of discovery, French ships had ventured round the Cape of Good Hope to ports in Sumatra in search of spices. One adventurer was Fr. Thomas Stevens an English Jesuit who sailed from Lisbon to Goa in 1579. In 1586 the merchant ship of Capt. Thomas Cavendish, and in 1589 the *Edward Bonaventure* sailed up to Zanzibar. Their stay of three months in Zanzibar angered the Portuguese because as discoverers of the spice route they thought they owned the route as well. By 1588 the English felt free to sail the world.

A Dutchman, Jan van Linschoten had spent five years working as a clerk for the Portuguese Archbishop of Goa. In 1596 the Dutch made their entry into the Indian Ocean helped by Jan van Linschoten's *Itinerario* relating the best months for sailing according to the Monsoons. The Dutch preferred to do their spice trade with Java and even though they had established a settlement in Mauritius in 1598 they chose instead to develop a stop on the African continent called Kaapstad (Cape Town). At this time an Anglo-Dutch alliance was formed in the interest of defeating the Portuguese stranglehold on the Indian Ocean trade.

Tomé Pirès a Portuguese sailor wrote of trade relations with the East African coast between Europe, Arabia and the Far East:

> This trade is carried out by ships from Aden and Cambay, many of one and many of the other. As the Kingdom of Cambay had the trade with Malacca, people from Macaris and people from Cairo, many Arabs chiefly from Aden, Abyssinians, Persians from Ormuz used to accompany the Gujeratis there in their ships. There were many of these in Malacca and many people from the Kingdom of the Deccan. The trade of Cambay is extensive. (Written in Malacca where he lived, 1512-1515).

It was in this period (16th century) that European countries were looking for markets for their goods. The French rounded the Cape in 1529, the English in 1580, the Dutch also in 1580. Under the competition Portuguese domination collapsed. They only managed to retain Goa on the west coast of India, Malacca in Malaysia, Timor in Indonesia, Angola in West Africa and Mozambique in East Africa.

The only two serious contenders for the East African trade were the Dutch and the English. The English were the only ones who survived and that was because of their British Indian subjects whom they claimed to 'protect' against exploitation and whose trading activities benefited British trade.

In the early years of European trading activity in Zanzibar, India held the lead in the volume of trade, but by 1830 onwards the share of western nations in it increased steadily, starting with the Americans then the French and Germans, and Britain through their British Indian subjects. After British and Portuguese colonization of the East African coast, 1800-

1806, Indian trade with Africa diminished. The British formed the East India Company and other colonial powers Belgium and Germany competed for trade. Indian trade only revived with the coming of the Imams of Muscat to Zanzibar, especially with Seyyid Said's permanent settlement in Zanzibar in 1843.

With the American Revolution of 1776 and independence from British monopoly on trade, came the American trader from Massachusetts, 'bold men of business, first rate ship builders, skilled navigators'. American shipmen were soon known at Calcutta, Bombay, Madras and Rangoon, Burma. Of the 80 ships that called at Zanzibar in 1859, thirty-five were American. For thirty years the Americans maintained their lead over all other contenders. In *merikani* the Africans obtained the commodity they most wanted. Other goods were tools, nails, mirrors and luxury articles.

The demand for *merikani* among the Africans increased so much that American merchants carried whole shiploads of it and the whole consignment was bought by Indian merchants and stored for sale in their warehouses. Besides *merikani* from America that had captured the African market, German muskets, hardware, rough crockery, cutlery and wire appeared in East Africa. Of direct British trade there was none, but British business shared in the British Indian trade since some of the cotton goods were of British manufacture. Sir Bartle Frere remarked:

> Lately there is increasing American, German and French trade and much interest in mercantile and political economies. German attention is directed towards the East African coast. Notwithstanding the large increase in trade that has grown up, Indian trade continues to grow.

Nearly all the trade of Zanzibar was in the hands of British Indian subjects, Bohoras, Banyans and Khojas some of whom were very wealthy. Dr. Livingstone was upset because:

> . . . all the valuable trade is lost to British merchants because until there is postal communication with Zanzibar it is impossible to compete with foreigners whose vessels arriving with the latest state of the market, are enabled to regulate their purchases and

> sales. The American, French and German merchants conduct nearly all their activities through those natives of India.

The activities of Indian merchants together with European and American traders, contributed to the rise of Zanzibar which became the chief market of the world for ivory, gum copal and cloves. British Consul Rigby reported, 'The trade of the port with India is becoming very important'. But it was not only Indian trade that brought importance to Zanzibar, it was more importantly the trade that the Indian generated with other parts of the world that put Zanzibar on the world map. Indian traders were extended credit up to six months by European traders. Indians bought entire cargoes from French, German and American merchants.

Sir Bartle Frere commented:

> Whenever there is any foreign trade it passes through Indian hands. European merchants buy and sell with the aid and advice of a *banyan* who is more like a partner than a mere broker, agent or go-between.

General Rigby further remarked that the Indian merchant had acquired his reputation through 'punctuality of payment and probity'.

If Zanzibar had become the great entrepôt for the whole of East Africa it was primarily Indian capital that was responsible for this transformation. Indian houses of trade supplied the entire coastline with merchandise from overseas and imported into Zanzibar products of the interior which they warehoused until a favourable opportunity arose for sale and shipment abroad. In this way Zanzibar became the great warehouse of the whole of East Africa. Its population possessed valuable elements of commerce in the wealthy and numerous settlers from India.

Indian trade can be divided into two phases. Up to 1750, when the European trading companies played only a marginal role. After 1750, when European trading companies helped the expansion of the market, furthered the process of capital accumulation by Indian merchants and promoted the subjugation of the Indian peasantry to produce low price exportable raw materials to advance the European Industrial Revolution.

Ready money was the means which enabled the Europeans to

penetrate the Indian trade network. The real superiority lay not in technology or the ability to create capital by free enterprise, free trade or open competition, but by the creation of monopolies. India continued to be the main manufacturing center especially for textiles. However Indian traders were eventually displaced from the internal trade by the East India Company's domination through unfair means and force.

The entry of Europeans to the Indian Ocean brought western-type merchant capitalism followed by industrial capitalism. There was also the urge among Europeans to capture markets of finished products from India and China, and primary agrarian and mineral commodities from Africa. For the Indian in general things did not improve. Europe's Industrial Revolution funded by trade with their colonies in East Africa and India, worked adversely for the population. In India, English manufactures stifled the muslin trade of Bengal by buying cheap raw materials from India and selling it back to India duty free, mass produced on power looms as Lancashire cottons.

The Indian merchant class was the dominant group in the trade network. With their maritime knowledge and experience of the various media of exchange, they were able to exert their influence since they controlled most firms of commerce. By the 18th century Bombay became the storehouse for East African, Arabian and Persian commerce. The trading firms of other imperialist nations in Europe and North America were allowed to carry on trading in Zanzibar as long as they did not threaten British interests. The influence of Indian merchants continued but that influence was bound to be reduced by measures amenable to British industrial capital whose rule was direct through the Zanzibar State.

If India had little to celebrate with the inclusion of Europeans in the Indian Ocean trade and particularly Indian trade, the Portuguese who were instrumental in 'opening the sea route to India' were even worse off. They had lost Mombasa and Fort Jesus, built to last as a symbol of 'everlasting Christian supremacy', to the heathens. Portugal was occupied by Philip II of Spain. Remoteness from the motherland discouraged many Portuguese from going back to Portugal. Living a life of idleness in Goa and calling themselves 'gentlemen' while they were nothing but peasants and tradesmen at home, who 'refuse to pay their bills in the Hindu shops'.

The Portuguese were not the only ones to yield to the temptations of power in the East. The Dutch and English quickly discovered easy access to luxury and money. It would be worth remembering that Queen

Elizabeth I (1559-1603) when giving her blessing to the East India Company exhorted them to 'adventure after merchandize, gold, pearl, jewels and other commodities, which are to be bought, bartered, procured, exchanged or otherwise obtained.' It is undeniable that commerce with India had done wonders for England's prosperity and made London a financial center. Men from humble beginnings rose to high political and social positions through fortunes made from trade in India.

Thomas Pitt an unlicensed trader, became Governor of Madras. His son William Pitt the Elder and his grandson William Pitt the Younger, became Prime Ministers of England. Sir William Mackinnon, a Scots millionaire who had started life as a grocer's clerk emigrated to India, made a fortune there in trade and founded an Indian Ocean shipping line, the British Indian Steam Navigation Company (B.I.S.N.Co.).

However the English were not the only ones who made fortunes through trade in India. Elihu Yale, a Bostonian and New England trader who also went to India to trade, became Governor of Madras and with the wealth accumulated in India he founded the prestigious Yale University.

Unfortunately European traders who engaged in trade in East Africa were not so lucky or prudent. They embarrassed the Government by going into 'unopened areas' especially Dick and West who used porter transport to trade between the Kenya coast and the Lake. Dick was killed by the Maasai and West was killed by the Nandi. Then there was John Boyes a leading European trader in portage trade, who fancied himself 'King of the Wakikuyu'. He was killed in 1899.

Chapter 13

The Indented Indian

The indenture system differs from slavery in this respect: Civil Rights left to the slave are the exception, while in the case of indentured labour it is the exceptions of which he is deprived. Hence the freedom of the slave is the bondage of the indentured labourer.
(The British Guyana Commission of 1871)

The voyages of discovery ushered in a new era of expansion of European civilization throughout the world. The Spanish, Portuguese, Dutch, French and English entered the field of colonial expansion from the 16th century onwards with the object of stimulating trade and wherever possible exploiting the natural resources of the new areas they occupied. To meet their labour requirements slaves from Africa were taken especially to North and South America. But with the gradual abolition of slavery (1807-1873) there arose an urgent need for cheap and controlled labour.

The coming of Europeans to the Indian Ocean brought western domination based on merchant capitalism, followed by industrial capitalism. The 'New World' created a plantation agriculture that required cheap labour, preferably slave labor. The opening up of Africa was followed closely by its colonization by European powers who lost no time in exploiting the resources of their respective carved out colonies in Africa.

European colonial powers continued to experience difficulties with African labour. The British and French did not realize the 'political significance' of the African resistance to colonial labour. It had nothing to do with laziness as they suspected, for in West Africa cocoa farmers, in Tanganyika coffee growers and in Uganda cotton growers, who were all

African, worked hard and prospered.

With the abolition of slavery in British colonies in 1834 and in French colonies in 1839, there arose an urgent need for labour in the various cotton, tobacco, sugar and other plantations of the British Empire. In 1834 the Government of India abolished the legal status of slavery, consequently 'indentured' labour replaced slavery, a similar system in practice but in theory it was paid labour, however little or unjust.

The British Government did not have to look further than India where millions of unemployed and impoverished peasants were eager for employment. To meet their labour requirements, private recruiting companies were established in Bombay and Karachi. These included the East India Company.

As early as 1830 a merchant from Bourbon (Réunion) imported 130 artisans from Calcutta (India) to work in the colony. A few more were brought in with their womenfolk in 1835. Indian convicts banished for life by the British Government were also being used in Mauritius to build roads. British economic interests demanded the employment of labourers from abroad, preferably India which provided cheap and efficient labour.

In 1807 Robert Farquhar first Governor of Mauritius, formerly Administrator of the East India Company, who at first was averse to slavery, nevertheless advocated the importation of slaves into Mauritius for the sugar plantations. He argued that the Abolition Act did not apply to Mauritius since it was acquired by the British after the Act was passed in Zanzibar. However when slavery was abolished worldwide in 1833, he had to look elsewhere for cheap labour. Following the example of Réunion which had imported 130 artisans from India, the 'experiment' on indenture was first carried out in Mauritius. Hence boatloads of Indian contract labourers began arriving in Mauritius.

The early shipments of indentured Indians resulted from agreements between commercial houses in Calcutta (British) and Pondicherry (French) and their British and French associates in Mauritius. It was essentially a private labour importation scheme between the employer and migrant worker, and the Government had no part in it at this time. They entered into a 'voluntary contract of service', a compromise between slavery and the free market system.

In 1834 the earliest emigration of labourers from Bihar, India, to various parts of the world beginning with Madagascar, Mauritius, Réunion and the West Indies, began. As the shareholders required maximum profits often unscrupulous methods were used to obtain labour cheaply. This included 'white servitude' where tempting offers of employment were made; free passage and a seven-year contract, at the end of which grants of land were promised to those who wished to remain in the country as 'free settlers' after the expiry of their contract. But they were in fact manipulated servants in the interest of the company.

From a small number of Indians introduced into Mauritius in 1834 or 1835 the number increased so considerably by 1837 that it attracted the attention of the British colonial Government. In 1838 the Government transmitted to Mauritius an order that 'contracting' labourers would be bound by the laws of the Colony.

The new type of 'slavery' under the guise of indenture was first undertaken as an experiment in Mauritius. In order to demonstrate that the migrants were not involuntary labourers, *Contracts and Wages of Indenture* were drawn up by British administrators along with numerous other regulations to ensure the 'protection' of the field hands. In reality, the lives of these immigrant workers were controlled by the all-encompassing indenture contracts which regulated:

> Working hours - sixteen a day, seven days a week, so that even weddings had to take place at night.
> Lodgings - separate for men and women even married couples.
> Medical treatment - each estate had its own facility and even though inadequate, had to be used.
> Duration of stay - three years, renewable for another three.
> Penalty - 1 ½ days' pay cut for each day of absence.

The pay was also fixed for the entire contract of indenture at the time of signing, no change. The 'hill coolies' were given a monthly wage of Rs 5.00 plus rations of rice, spices and *ghee* (clarified butter). The document was drawn up between the *dangurs* or hill coolies or tribals, and the company. By 1839 thousands of Indians were imported into Mauritius, first as slaves and then as indentured workers.

The first batch of indentured labour called 'coolie trade' arrived from India in 1839. This particular contingent came from southern India and was consigned both to Mauritius and South Africa. The British capitalists had a share in this operation. James Blyth chartered ships to carry coolies and rice, thus making a double profit.

By 1837 there were 20,000 labourers in Mauritius and by 1843 the number increased to 60,000. Few of the 'hill coolies' found their way home in spite of a three-year contract. Injustices prevailed, for instance by 1840 due to the inefficiency of the local freed slave population who were now employed as 'apprentices' while they were being replaced with labour from India, the wage bill rose, so that plantation owners were unable to pay wages as well as repay loans. Consequently wages of the indentured labourers had to wait. Their three-year contract was extended to five without notice and without any monetary increase.

Nevertheless Indians imported to work on Mauritian sugar plantations worked conscientiously and kept the terms of their contract. It was through Indian indentured labour that Mauritius became more and more important on the world market as the primary sugar exporter. According to S. B. Mukerji, sugar output grew from 11,200 metric tons in 1828 to 500,000 metric tons in 1953. Sir Charles Bruce, the Governor, was disappointed to find that India and not Britain was the main importer of Mauritian sugar.

The first batch of free immigrants to Mauritius arrived in December 1923. Most of them had worked in Fiji, Surinam, Natal and Trinidad. The new immigrants were treated no better than indentured labourers since that was the level of labour required in the country. They complained bitterly about being duped into conditions unsuitable to their 'castes'. Brahmins and Kshatriyas because of their caste superiority had never touched a pickaxe in their lives. Nevertheless there was also praise for them.

> It's thanks to Indian labour that we have obtained such good harvests today. The Indian is an intelligent and thrifty worker who loves the earth. Of docile character he adapts himself easily to the customs of the country and remains faithful to his employer. (Pierre de Sornay in *Le Cereen*, 1932)

Some British newspapers protested that the lives of these migrant workers were no better than slaves'. But the time was soon to come when pity would turn to envy, when the labourers climbed out of their abject poverty to make Mauritius into a 'little India beyond the sea'.

With the introduction of indentured labourers who were mostly Hindus, began the arrival of Muslim and Chinese traders in Mauritius. By 1907 the Cutchi Memons had established five trading houses, the Muslims acquired a monopoly of the provision and textile trade. Of the 47 registered traders, nine were Hindus and six Chinese.

In mainland Africa indentured labour went to East and South Africa, other immigrants came on their own, they had heard of Indian merchants who first came in the 1800s. As migrant workers they gave little trouble to the British. They undertook unpleasant tasks and insulated the British from direct contact with the Africans.

The early planters in South Africa experienced great difficulty in securing labour. In Natal, settlers mainly from Britain struggled to find a profitable basis of economic exploitation. In the 1850s it became apparent that there was a future for sugarcane plantations along the coast, but they lacked the manpower. Labour was essential especially for the new sugar plantations. Africans were not used to wage labour under plantation conditions. They then turned to indentured labour from India which had already supplied labour to Mauritius. These workers made the fortunes of the sugar plantation owners.

India's earliest contact with South Africa dates back to 1860 when the Crown Colony of Natal secured the first 120,000 labourers by indenture from India 'to fill a dire need' for its sugar, tea and other plantations requiring careful tillage. Labour was recruited by agents in India for a period of three years, a practice already underway in the British territories of Mauritius, Trinidad, Jamaica and Guyana. However in South Africa there was opposition from Europeans other than sugar planters, consequently importation of labour from India came to a standstill and so did the sugarcane cultivation.

In 1874 £10,000 per year for twenty years was allotted by the government towards the cost of importing Indian indentured labour for Natal. Labour was recruited by agents in Bombay and Karachi on terms agreed upon by the Government of India for a period of three years. The Mauritian system formed the basis for the Natal system with the offer of either returning to India or settling in South Africa as 'free immigrants' on a small plot of land. These Indian settlers who became labourers and farmers, planted sugarcane and raised fruit and vegetables, others engaged in trade.

Cape Province received 20,000 and Transvaal 10,000 indentured labourers for the tea and sugar plantations and other crops. The South African Indians engaged in a variety of occupations. They were not only traders but agriculturists as well. In the Transvaal Indians also mined coal, laid railway lines and planted fruit and vegetables.

In the Cape Province as well as the Transvaal Indians engaged in trade and commerce and brought trade goods to remote areas. However the Government restricted licenses to traders in order to protect European traders who were just getting into trade at this time.

In South Africa there was a subsidized repatriation scheme, but of the 143,000 Indians who came to South Africa, only 27,000 returned to India. Mahatma Gandhi lived in South Africa for many years where he founded the Natal Indian Congress in 1894. In 1906 and 1914 Gandhi's son Manilal edited the newspaper *Indian Opinion*, he was also leader of the passive resistance movement against apartheid in 1952.

In East Africa indentured labour went mainly to Kenya, Uganda and Tanganyika. In Kenya and Uganda the British needed labour to build the railway. In Tanganyika the Germans imported some indentured labour from India, but they were able to mobilize quite a sizable labour force from the local African population for their sisal plantations.

It was towards the end of the 19th century that the British Government in Africa negotiating with the British government in India, began to indenture large numbers of Indians to build the Uganda Railway in East Africa. In 1896 the first batch of Indian indentured labour arrived in Mombasa for the construction of the railway from Mombasa to Lake Victoria Nyanza. Of the 32,000 indentured men mainly from Punjab, 6,534 were sent back to India as invalids in just one year, 2,493 died during the construction of the railway (1896-1901), 12,644 were hospitalized with injuries (some of whom may also have died) and only 10,329 opted to stay on in Kenya and Uganda.

Worldwide, indentured labour went to Mauritius, Réunion Madagascar, Kenya, Uganda and Tanganyika in East Africa. Natal, Cape Province and Transvaal in South Africa. Trinidad, Jamaica, Caribbean Basin, British Guyana and Surinam in South America; Malaysia, Rangoon in Burma and Fiji. Between 1640 and 1917 about two million Indians were transported out of India, first as slaves and later as indentured labour for the construction and transportation industry. Of the total number of indentured labourers imported into Africa by 1903, nearly 8% died and

20% returned to India. By 1917 indentured labour slowly began to end and by 1926 it was effectively abolished.

History should not deny the Indian contribution to the development and prosperity of Britain's colonial empire in the 19th century. Separated from their native land the immigrants proved to be the hardy pioneers that triumphed over all adversities, most particularly the hostilities of the white man. In *The Immigrant Coolie* Ranji Nowbath describes how Indians became part of world history although they received little attention from world historians.

> They will never be able to eradicate the knowledge of the extreme pain which the immigrant *coolies* suffered and deny the heavy price they paid with their life's blood so that their descendents may live in comfort and decency.

Chapter 14

The Uganda Railway

> **Men would die during the building of the railway and men would live because of it. Famine would be a thing of the past and because of it towns would be built - and cities too.**
> (Edward Rodwell in *Coast Causerie*, 1972)

The old trading routes of the East African trade played a vital part in settlement, which also resulted in the Uganda Railway. At the time of the construction of the railway Kenya did not exist. The territory was known as British East Africa hence the name Uganda Railway, sometimes called 'Mombasa-Uganda Railway'. The Uganda Railway was to help kill the slave trade and develop the territories it served (Rodwell, 1972). There was no place called Nairobi either, the settlement had its beginnings as a shanty town for railway men to rest and recuperate before the next onslaught.

A decision to construct a railway 'upon Indian methods and chiefly by means of Indian *coolies* was taken in 1895.' (*Final Report on the Uganda Railway*, edition 2164, 1904, pp.7). In October 1895 the Indian Emigration Act of 1893 was legalized to implement the recruitment of Indian labour for the building of the Uganda Railway. Nearly 32,000 labourers and artisans plus 5,000 subordinate employees were contracted for three years. These included stone masons, iron smiths, carpenters, plate layers and wheel wrights, all highly skilled in their own field (Kotecha,1994).

> I wonder if in England the importance of one aspect of the construction has been realized. It means fifteen thousand *coolies* some hundreds of Indian clerks, draftsmen, mechanics, surveyors and policemen. The

> Indian Penal Code, Indian postal system, Indian coinage, clothing, right across the wastes, deserts, forests and swamps. (Sir Harry Johnston).

Two British surveyors from India, Macdonald and Pringle were appointed to prepare a feasibility study report on the possibility of constructing the railway. Forty-six Indian experts made a survey to assess the cost which would be borne by the British Government of India from taxes paid mainly by Indian traders!

Capt. Macdonald who had a good deal of experience in railway building reported to the Bombay office and after careful consideration decided to 'rely on men of whose worth he had personal knowledge.' His staff consisted of Capt. Pringle, Lt. Twining and Lt. Austin and forty-six Indian surveyors. And although Sir Frederick Jackson calls them *kalassies* they were actually trained Indian surveyors.

The man chosen to build the railway in East Africa was George Whitehouse (later knighted), Chief Engineer and Manager. He had worked on railways in Natal (South Africa), Mexico, Peru and India and after the Uganda Railway, on the Central Argentine Railway. Whitehouse, drew heavily on his Indian experience and connections. He secured the services of two Indian officers of the Indian Public Works Department (PWD) who in turn recruited 2,000 coolies and a number of masons, carpenters, surveyors and draftsmen. The cost per man was Rs.30 per month, excluding repatriation, rations and medical expenses.

The view, although beautiful from Mombasa was depressing from an engineer's perception with its thick vegetation and undergrowth. British railway engineers brought to Mombasa from India were appalled by the geographical obstacles. The project had extraordinary difficulties, it was a 'mountain railway' constructed on 3.28 gauge. At Mombasa the route crossed a ½ mile long bridge (now a causeway) to the mainland. Starting at about 200 ft. above sea level, for the first 200 miles the track lay always on the ascent. The route had to be hacked through forest and bush to Nairobi at 5,459 ft., then 9,000 ft. to Uplands, dropping a little to a 7,000 ft. plateau into the Rift Valley to 1,500 ft., climbing again to 4,600 ft. to the Kikuyu Escarpment and finally falling 3,720 ft. to Lake Victoria, the last three elevations in 90 miles. It must be mentioned here, that despite all the obstacles the Indian engineering staff, who carried the major work load served well and loyally, one died in Kenya.

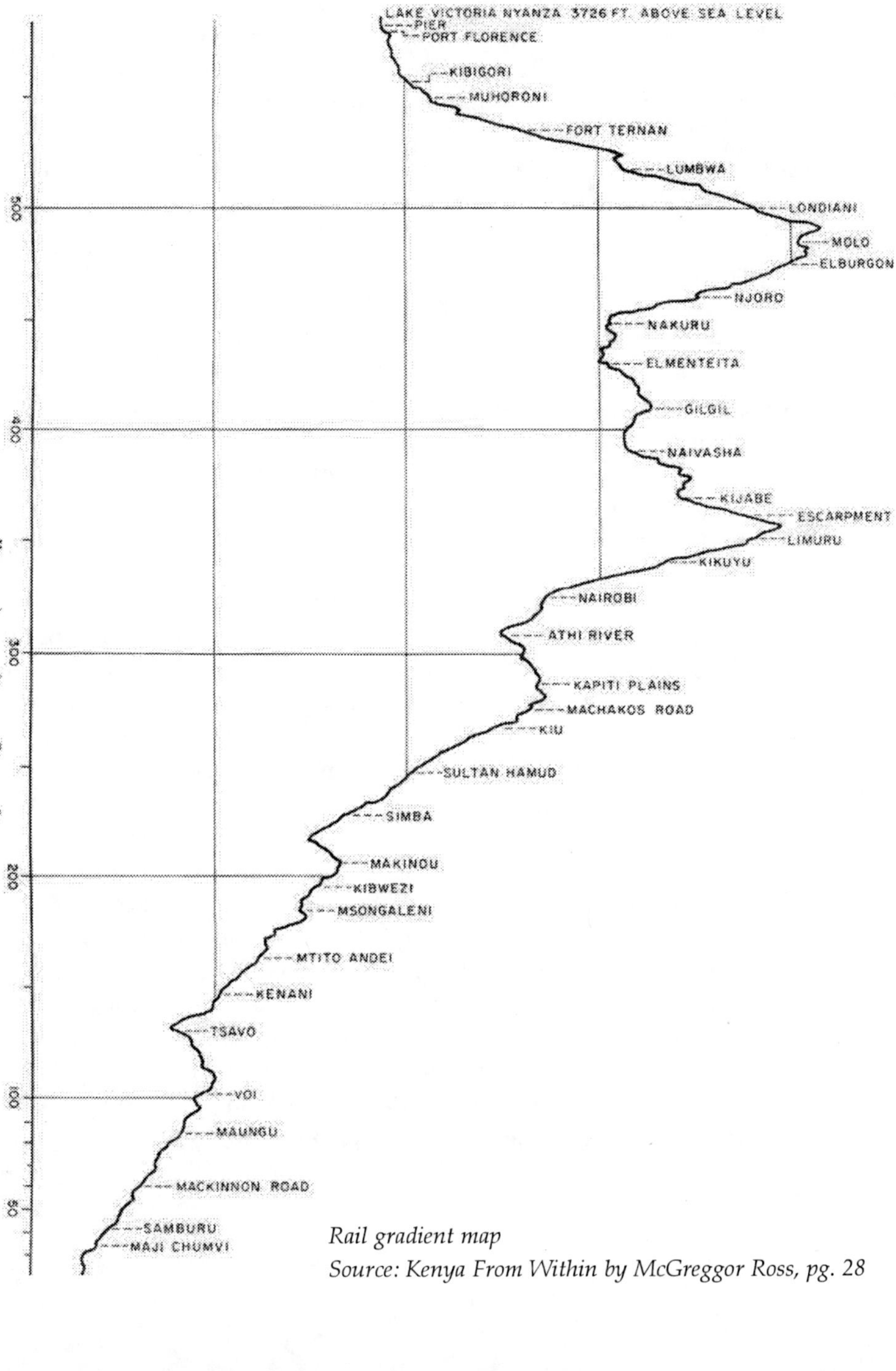

Rail gradient map
Source: Kenya From Within by McGreggor Ross, pg. 28

In 1895 A.M. Jeevanjee was asked to contact Cowasji Dinshaw & Co. in Aden in connection with using his ships for transporting material for the building of the Uganda Railway. Jeevanjee's firm was hired by the Uganda Railway to recruit Indian construction workers to erect temporary buildings, for rock cuttings and other earthworks. On 3, January 1896, 32,000 workers under indenture arrived from India to begin work on the railway, 18,000 were mainly from Punjab. Their number included masons, carpenters, ironsmiths, clerks, surveyors, draftsmen. A coolie's monthly wage was Rs 12, and a stone mason's was Rs 45 per month. Karim Bux a genuine stone mason and skilled craftsman but no longer young, was down graded to coolie on account of others posing as stone masons, because of the higher pay. By May 1896 it was reported that the Uganda Railway was going ahead at a cost of £3 million, loaned by the Imperial Government.

By late 1896 not a sleeper had been laid (*The Times*). Eleven hundred coolies at a monthly wage of Rs 12 and artisans from India were on the spot, and a thousand more expected. The Indian workers were backed by armies of African porters and labourers. Plate-laying began on the mainland on 4, August 1896. Then came the Taru desert with not a drop of water. The earth was dense with thorny jungle which would not burn readily and clearing was necessary to draw the vegetation clear of the tracks. In spite of all the difficulties less than a year after the first rails had been laid on mainland Mombasa, sixty-five miles of the distance to Nairobi had been completed and wagons used to carry goods.

However one should not proceed without mentioning the man in charge of the work force, Robert Turk. He became an 'engineer' with 'eleven years of experience working on the harbour at Madras and the bridge on the Godavari river'. He had learnt about concrete and steel, coolies and the Hindustani language. Now he was in the Taru Desert building the Uganda Railway. Ibrahim was his chief headman in charge of the building gang 'a ferocious master with enjoyment of beating'.

Whitehouse had abandoned his timetable. In Kilindini it had seemed feasible, and an optimum rate of progress had been calculated. But these 'men of Madras and southern India, the Pathans and Punjabis, had brought indolence and apathy, they were prone to accident and prey to zymotic disease. They were a long way from home they moved slowly into inertia'.

> The Taru Desert was heat filled, fierce, the caravan fell silent, each man cocooned in his own sheath of effort, there would only be the rasp of breath and the scuff of feet. They moved jerkily with uncoordinated movements. The flesh of face, arm and calf black against their white clothes. They were in distress, agape with thirst, saturated with sweat. Many of them knelt before the thorn-boles slicing in desperation at the stubborn wood. Others bent in the immobility of exhaustion and spittle hung from their mouths. They begged for water but since they were not Turk's responsibility he refused.
>
> In the evening they trailed back to railhead their feet torn by the spires, the blood leaving a spoor. The water had dried in the holes and those that contained some, was foul smelling. Men sickened from the sun, sat or squatted in the shade of the coaches. There were seven hospital tents where men lay with limbs as thin and as yellow as celery, with the sun in their brains and maggots in their toes. (Hardy, 1965).

Manpower was continually drained away through disease, exhaustion and attacks from wild animals. The animals employed were unused to local conditions. Camels and horses perished, oxen could not be used because of the tsetse fly. Donkeys were the only animals that proved satisfactory, but in short supply.

In March 1898 arrived Lieutenant Colonel J. H. Patterson, a decorated member of the Distinguished Service Order (DSO) an engineer with a Foreign Office appointment. His first job was to survey the work already in progress, that is, after he 'surveyed' his staff of four personal servants. A cook, a Sikh *jamnadar* (bodyguard), the other two looked after his personal needs. For instance his bath water had to be a precise temperature - or else. He demanded respect, cleanliness and obedience. Virtue would be rewarded, lapses punished.

The dangers the railway workers faced were many. Crocodiles lay in wait for the man who went to the river to collect water. He could be bitten by poisonous snakes or devoured by python, gored by buffalo or stalked by hyenas. In the rainy season mudslides buried many labourers digging in the trenches. Then came a series of disasters. An epidemic of bubonic plague in India disorganized the supply of labour. In British East Africa there was a severe outbreak of malaria and blackwater fever among railway staff and labour. Every European had fever at some time. Indian workers seemed more resistant at first but later sickened with malaria. Jiggers, pests and the tsetse fly played havoc with men and animals. And of course the man-eating lions kept the labourers in a constant state of terror. The danger became so great that work stopped for three weeks.

> Now the bravest of men in the world will not stand constant terror of this sort indefinitely. They had come from India to work for the Government not to supply food for either lions or devils. (Colonel Patterson, 1907).

In June 1900 Charles Henry Ryall was killed by a man-eating lion at Kima. He was taken off the stationery guard coach before midnight. A hunt for the beast was organized and a reward of £100 was offered by Sir George Whitehouse, Chief Engineer of the Uganda Railway. Ryall's mother also offered a reward of £100 for the capture of the beast dead or alive. The brute was captured in a cunningly devised trap set by Costello (read Castello) a locomotive foreman at Makindu and Roderigues, fitter-chargeman (Foran, 1962).

Colonel Patterson, Dr. Brough and *jamnadar* Rasul Khan, the gun bearer, organized a round-the-clock patrol. One night the colonel saw two lions and with faultless aim he shot one but the other escaped into hiding. The lion was stalked and shot by *jamnadar* Rasul on 30, January 1899. (Kotecha, 1994).With less than 200 miles of track completed the £ 3 million had been spent.

> Yet there was no wavering, as soon as a new stretch of track was laid the locomotives snorted forward through terrain no white man had seen twenty years ago. The eventual triumph of the 'Lunatic Line' at a cost of more than five million pounds, entrenched British colonialism in East Africa' (Hall, 1996).

The British Parliament complained about the rising cost of the railway, so the Uganda Railway management decided to effect economies by reducing privileges and allowances of lower level white staff. The result was a strike of white employees in Mombasa.
A Report in the official history of the Company states:

> A few agitators got out of hand and persuaded some Indian *coolies* to follow their example. Some damage was done to property, rails were pulled up and work came to a standstill. (Marshall).

The strike was disorganized for lack of a Union to supply the needs of the strikers who were isolated in their tents while others worked. Whitehouse dismissed the militants and settled the grievances of the more conciliatory.

Nairobi, the goal of the last three years was reached in 1899. The Indian railway workers were welcomed by the Indian traders who had already set up shops in the area.

> There was the site which within half a century was to become the capital of Kenya, a city in a country developed and maintained by a railway which turned waste territory into a land with great potential. (Rodwell, 1972).

> The influence of the railway is most marked even on the unpromising region, local people in contact with it have already commenced to trade and a demand for goods is springing up. Traders [Indian] are beginning to settle around the different stations and at Voi there is quite a flourishing bazaar.
> (Patterson, 1979).

The original Uganda Railway from Mombasa to Port Florence in Kisumu on Lake Victoria was opened on December 26, 1901 and from Jinja to Namasagali in 1910, and finally to Kampala in 1931. In the 20th century there is no other construction of this magnitude that could have been done entirely by hand, stone upon stone, girder after girder. And this includes the towering Tsavo bridge!

> But for the building of the Mombasa-Uganda Railway it would not have been possible for Europeans to penetrate the East African interior. And it was Indian labour which made the materialization of the seemingly 'lunatic' railway scheme feasible. (Sir John Kirk, 1910).

Even the committed imperialist Winston Churchill had this to say:

> It is by Indian labour that the one vital railway on which everything else depends, was constructed.

With the building of the Uganda Railway from Mombasa to Kisumu on Lake Victoria the British Government was anxious to generate traffic for its expensive railway. Cotton was already grown by Indians near the lake in Kavirondo.

> Experiments in cotton growing are already bearing fruit and there is no reason why East Africa should not be one of the greatest cotton producing countries of the world. (Sir Charles Eliot, 1905, former Lieutenant Governor of Bengal).

Accordingly the British Cotton Growers' Association was formed to promote cotton growing in the British Empire and to create taxable income.

New jobs were created throughout the colony, administrative jobs and jobs connected with the new railway. Besides needing clerical staff connected with the running of the railway there was need for catering personnel. J. A. Nazareth acted as official caterers to the Uganda Railways by providing chefs and other staff required both in the restaurant cars on the train as well as restaurants at the railway stations.

However the building of the railway was not the end of the hardships for the Indian stationmaster and linesmen living in the wilderness, each day brought its challenges. The single track railway line was sometimes used by buffalo, giraffe and zebra as a highway. On one instance the distraught stationmaster sent a telegram, 'Two lions on platform. Train approaching. Linesman on water tank. Cannot give signal. Please arrange matters.' (Kotecha, 1994).

In Suresh Joshi's words:

> In the gathering darkness all around there are threatening sounds, snakes hiss, sinister steps fall softly in the hollows, storm winds and rain come and go, every side there is desolation, the heart is crushed.

> There can be no doubt that the Indian community has in fact played an indispensable part in the development of these territories. Apart from the construction of the Kenya-Uganda Railway the services of the Indian artisans and mechanics have been widely used by the public at large.
> (Hilton Young Commission, 1927).

White officers involved in the building of the railway were anxious to record their experiences especially those like Major Macdonald, whose work was actually done by Indian surveyors. In 1897 he wrote a book describing his experiences as Chief Engineer of the preliminary survey of the Uganda Railway. But the book that is remembered to this day and much read, is that written by Lieutenant-Colonel J. H. Patterson 'who is better known for his encounter with lions than his engineering skills'. The first draft was sent to Theodore Roosevelt who suggested that '*The Man-eating Lions of Uganda*' should be preserved in permanent record. The book was eventually called *Man-eaters of Tsavo* and published in 1907.

Chapter 15

The Trading Winds

Around 120 BC members of the Egyptian Coast Guard found an Indian sailor shipwrecked on the Red Sea. They took him to Ptolemy VII. The sailor spoke a language that no one in Alexandria knew so Ptolemy ordered that the sailor be taught Greek. Thus educated the sailor taught his captors something amazing; the Monsoons over the Indian Ocean blow in a regular pattern - from northeast to southwest in winter and the opposite direction in summer.

(Strabo In *National Geographic* vol. 196, no. 2, August 1999)

The Trade Winds or Monsoons as they are called in the Indian Ocean, the prevailing northeasterly and southwesterly winds of the sub-tropics, derive their name from their constant course. The Trade Winds occupy two belts between latitudes 5 degrees north and 25 degrees south of the Equator. The Trade Winds are the most consistent wind system on earth. These winds were used to great advantage in the days of sailing for crossing the oceans for trade, hence the name (*Encyclopedia, Americana*,1958).

There is evidence of Indians making voyages across the open sea to East Africa from antiquity and of the Malays using the ocean currents to reach Madagascar. (Chandra, 1987). After the realization of the potential of the Monsoon winds Indians made direct voyages from Arabia to Madagascar which was settled by peoples of Indonesia over 2,000 years earlier. The Malagasy language includes Sanskrit words but its root is Malay.

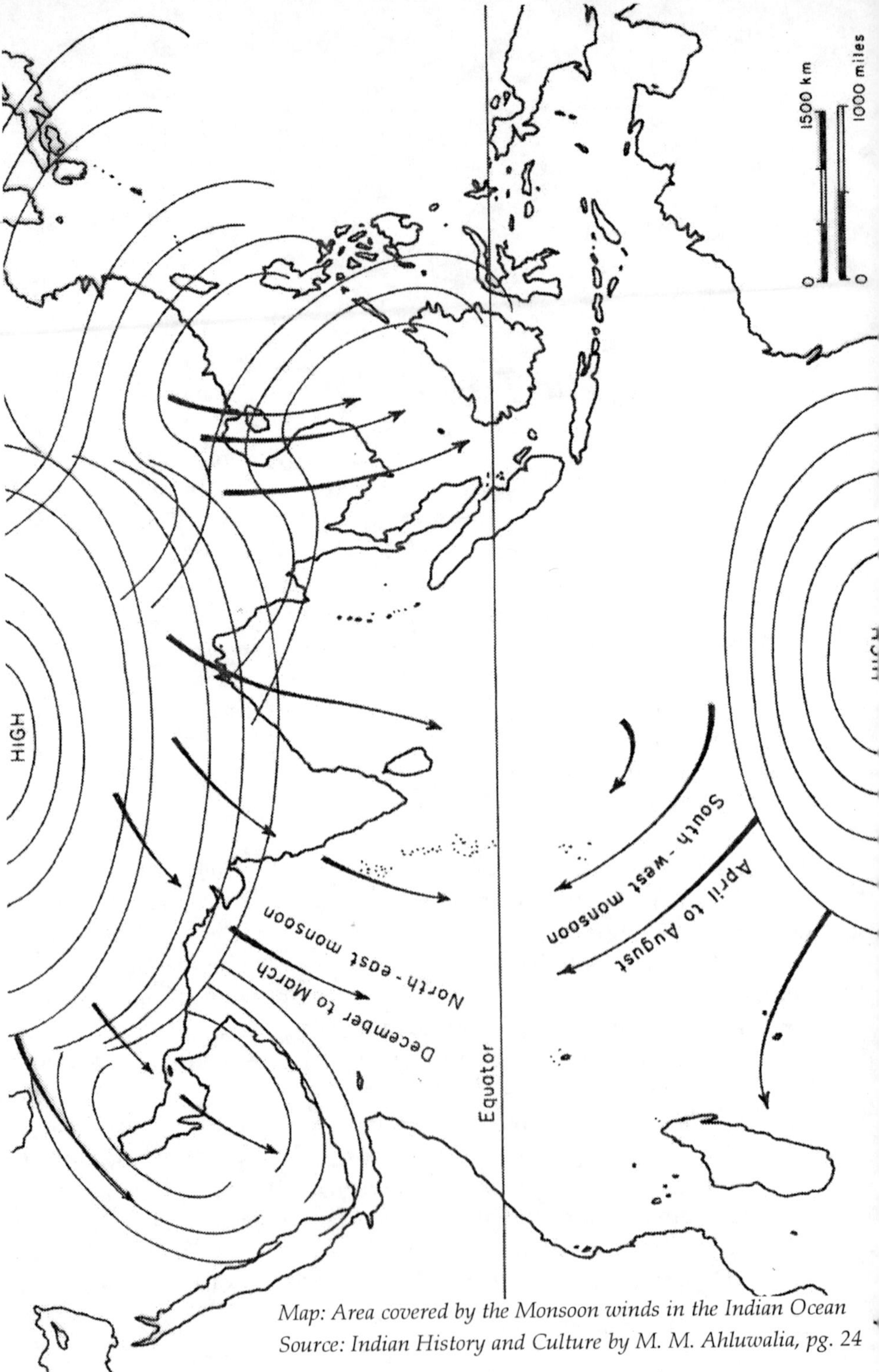

Map: Area covered by the Monsoon winds in the Indian Ocean
Source: Indian History and Culture by M. M. Ahluwalia, pg. 24

For centuries the Arabs and Indians knew how to use the Monsoon winds which blew their dhows northeast towards Africa from December to April and a few months later, May to September, changing direction to become the southwest Monsoons, taking them back to India (Marsh, 1961). The traders who came to East Africa with the northeast Monsoons were from India, Arabia, Indonesia, Persia, Ceylon and China. Pre-nineteenth century trade followed a triangular route; west coast of India, the Arabian coast, East African coast and back to India. It is believed that they had been trading with Africa for over 2,000 years. (Amier Haji Amier, 1992).

The whole traffic with other countries in those pre-steamer days was carried on in sailing ships called *dhows* or *gurabs, bhaglas* and *gangas.* The Indian ship-building industry was well organized and the ships' design was comparable even to those of the East India Company's of the 19th century. (Samson, 1993). These *dhows* were built in India and the Persian Gulf.

In India they had a very ancient traditional design. At first the boards were 'sewn' together with ropes made of coconut fibre. Nails were not used because of a superstition that the metal would be attracted towards the bottom of the sea. Later the boards were still 'sewn' together and sealed with a gum for which Mafia Isalnd on the East African coast, was an important source. (Samson, 1993). *Dhows* had pointed projecting prow and stern, single forward-sloping mast made of palm frond matting shaped in a square sail. They ranged from 30 to 50 tons, some that came from Surat ranged from 50 to 500 tons. *Bhaglas* and *ganga*s came from Cutch, they had square sterns, high poops and long prows, one or two palm matting masts, 50 to 60 tons reaching 160 tons. Even though they had their distinguishing marks the sailing ships came to be known by one name, dhow.

It was the Trade Winds that facilitated traffic in the Indian Ocean. Dhows used to come from and return to India 'in their proper seasons'. Those which came with the northeast Monsoons (*kaskazi*) in November/December from India, Muscat and the Benedir coast and returned in March/April were termed *Mosam* (Arabic) or *Avlani* (Gujerati). Those which came with the same northeast Monsoons but stayed longer and returned to India in June-August were known as *Dhamani.* Speed depended on catching the wind at its 'most suitable' strength.

Every November the Trade Winds or Monsoons blow from the north-

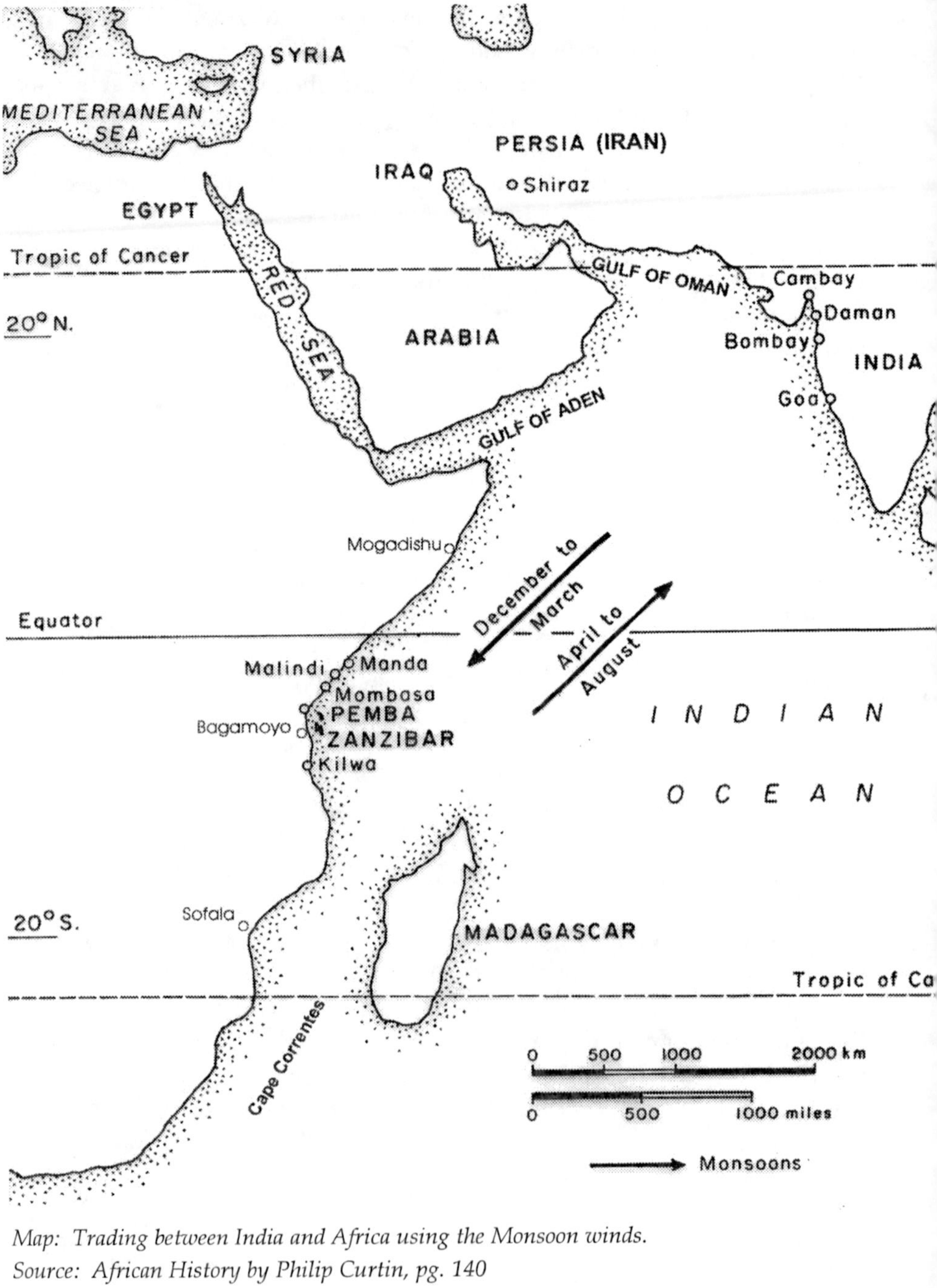

Map: Trading between India and Africa using the Monsoon winds.
Source: African History by Philip Curtin, pg. 140

east and continue blowing with remarkable steadiness till the end of March. Every April till September the process is reversed. The northeast Monsoons covering the Indian Ocean as far as Madagascar blow at the beginning of November, they are at their most forceful between December and March, becoming gentle till April. The southwest Monsoons beginning in April are strongest from June to September. Dhows could cover the 2,500 miles to India in 25-26 days at this time.

The western shore of the Indian Ocean follows a fairly straight line from Zanzibar. A strong wind blows from the south south-west following the mouth of the Gulf of Aden to the Gulf of Oman. At the Gulf of Oman it bends eastwards to the mouth of the Indus River and then south south-east down the length of western India. This phenomenon was known to the early sailors. Arabs 'hugged' the shore but the Indians trusted the winds to take them to Africa and bring them safely back home (Coupland, 1938) by September. From Zanzibar to the Gulf of Aden is 1,700 miles and to the Gulf of Oman is 2,000 miles. A direct route from Mombasa to Bombay would be 2,500 miles.

Indian Ocean trade was dictated by the Monsoons which allowed ships from India to reach East Africa between October and March. Return had to be between April and September. At first trading dhows went as far south as Sofala, which soon became unpopular as by the time the dhows reached Cape Correntes, beyond the Zambezi Delta and Sofala, the Monsoon winds petered out. Ships venturing beyond the Tropic of Capricorn would have to struggle back against the southwest *Agulhas* current.

> It has been said that the history of Zanzibar has been written by the wind. (Abdul Sharif & Ed Ferguson, Eds., 1991).

The pattern of winds favoured the northern coast of East Africa as a destination for overseas traders. The crucial question was how far south sailors could go before the northeast Monsoons lost their force, keeping in mind that the ships needed to leave by April for the return journey to India. Towards the end of the Monsoon season the wind blows only in the northern section of the East African coast, moving further north with each successive month. The northeasterlies blow as far as Mombasa in February but only as far as Somalia in March. Given the time constraints from the home port, Zanzibar was usually the southern limit for navigation. Hence Zanzibar became the preferred destination and major entrepôt. Mariners who wished to reach Kilwa in southern Tanganyika had to sail past Zanzibar by January and wait there till August when the wind changed to become the southwest Monsoons. Eventually Zanzibar became the chosen southernmost sailing limit and those who wished to collect goods from Kilwa had to travel in smaller boats, *jahazis* or *zambucos*, to collect them. Mombasa and Malindi although centrally positioned had poor hinterlands, which did not yield much trade goods.

East African coastal sailing continued most of the year, assembling goods for overseas markets. Towns north of Sofala on the Swahili coast acted as 'staging ports'. Kilwa was ideally placed to play the 'middleman role' where goods were brought from the interior of Africa to be transmitted by smaller boats to Zanzibar. Traders required ready goods for they could not stop long. These and other geographical factors shaped the history of trade with the east coast of Africa.

The discovery of the Monsoons is credited to *Hippalus*. According to Charles Vanderlinden *Hippalus* was not the name of any individual but of the Monsoons named by Indians. (Chandra, 1987). In AD 45 Roman sailors discovered the secret of the Monsoons and a little later in AD 50 or 60 the Greeks stumbled upon the knowledge. (Marsh,1961).

> If the wind called *Hippalus* happens to be blowing it is possible to arrive in forty days at the nearest mart in India called Muzuris (Mangalore). Indians who set sail at the beginning of *Typus* (December) can go and return in the same year carrying products of India, silk, cotton, cotton cloths, diamonds, precious stones, ginger, spices, ivory. Cotton was extremely rare for other countries except India. (*East Africa Today*, 1958-1959).

Chapter 16

Indians and the Slave Trade

Someone has to make the decision as to what is worth recording and as a result the history we read in our textbooks and other reference works is often skewed by bias, political slants, subjective notions and misinformation.

(Dougie Oakes, launching the Reader's Digest book *The Truth About History*)

Slavery existed in Africa for centuries. It was customary among chiefs to sell prisoners of war as slaves. However, if slavery had not advanced beyond the immediate domestic needs of Africa it would not have got out of hand.

Although some form of slavery had always existed in Africa slaving had never been more than a minor aspect of the East African trade and even with the coming of the Portuguese, slaves were not an important cargo. However the Slave Trade established by the Arabs especially on the east coast of Africa before the advent of the Portuguese prevented the spread of economic and political expansion especially among the coastal tribes. It kept the African interior in a chronic state of terror and inter-tribal warfare. Then from the 15th to the 19th centuries during European contact with East Africa, trade became 'unvoluntary'. The increased trade in slaves and ivory without introducing new means of production, upset the economy (Gupta, 1981).

Only nine years after Columbus' first trip across the Atlantic in 1492 the Spanish legalized the importation of slaves to its American colonies. In India, some extent of the Slave Trade from Africa is ascertained by the fact that the Muslim King of Gaur in Bengal (1459-1474) possessed some 8,000 slaves. There was also an influx of Abyssinians (Ethiopians) and other East Africans into western India in the 5th century AD. Although most of these *hashish* or *sidis* came as slaves, through faithfulness they rose to positions of trust in their owner's establishment. After slavery was abolished in India in 1873, these freed slaves known as *Sidis of Jangira* held much power in Ahmadnagar.

Regarding slavery in West Africa the testimony of the historian Sir Alan Burns is clear:

> Europeans went to West Africa in Elizabethan times to establish slave stations. By the slave trade they introduced, Benin and other ancient indigenous civilizations were undermined and the African will to resist was enfeebled or decayed. The European then established colonial rule in the 19th century for the ostensible purpose of suppressing the slave trade which their own citizens had conducted for 300 years and for which at one time Britain had the monopoly.

Slavery was inevitably followed by colonization by Europeans. The East African slave trade operated by Arabs was never on the scale that it became after the Europeans entered the trading market. Slave labour was in demand in the new colonies established by European nations, which they had converted to tropical plantation agriculture. In the 18th century the Dutch from Cape Province began to take slaves from Madagascar and Mozambique. They were followed by the French. In 1754 a Frenchman, Capt. Morice was buying slaves from the Sultan of Kilwa for the French seeking labour for their plantations in the Indian Ocean islands of Ile de France (Mauritius), Mascarene Islands and Bourbon (Réunion), as well as St. Dominique in Haiti.

In 1811 Capt. Thomas Smee travelled to Zanzibar as a representative of the Bombay Government. He gave a graphic description of the horrors of the slave trade and Indian involvement in it. Indian customs collectors charged Arab traders $1.00 per slave, while Christians were charged $10.00. Zanzibar had become the greatest slaving port in East Africa. In 1859 no less than 19,000 slaves left from that island.

Unfortunately for the Indians British explorers also tried to implicate them in the slave trade. Dr. Livingstone denounced them seriously as sabotaging his efforts against the trade by keping slaves for domestic use.

These accusations were refuted by Speke, Rigby and Kirk. Ironically the British firm of Fraser and Company, the largest single slave exporters under Commander Fraser of the British Navy, were not similarly accused by Livingstone.

Dr. Livingstone waged a grim struggle against the slave trade. His dream for a 'legitimate commerce' which would replace the traffic in humanity and teach the Africans to develop their own resources, never faded. Dr. Livingstone was asked if the increase in indigenous commercial trade would lessen the interest in the slave trade.

> The export of able bodied laborers from the country deters free laborers from coming to settle in Zanzibar or along the coast because they would not be safe even for a day.

Parvan Sharma says, 'For propaganda purposes they (British) relied on Dr. David Livingstone's report presented to the British Parliament in 1872'. The Report said:

> The *banians* of Zanzibar who are proteceted British subjects carry on the Slave Trade in Central Africa. The Arabs and *banians* hate me and dread exposure. The trading system called *Cutchee* or *Banian* trading consists of marauding and murdering by Arabs at the instigation of British Indian subjects who cunningly secure all the profits.

Indian awareness of the slave trade cannot be denied since they exercised such a predominant influence over East African trade. Indians had their own ships and dhows as carriers of their merchandise between Zanzibar and the coast of Arabia. Unfortunately their vessels were also hired for the illicit trade in slaves and many slaves made their way through this means to Arabia and even India.

Indians were indirectly implicated in the slave trade inasmuch as Indian merchant capital was financing both movements, in and out of the interior of Africa, where manufactured goods found their way into the interior to be exchanged for slaves and ivory. Indians were involved in the slave trade because they advanced goods and money, supplied muskets and gun powder bought from European and American mechants, to caravans that bartered the cloth and utensils required by the tribal chiefs in exchange for slaves, ivory and gum copal.

Indians were directly connected with the slave trade through the customs collection since slaves were a regular and direct source of revenue supplied to the Sultan of Zanzibar who farmed the customs collection to an Indian who most certainly knew of the nature of the 'cargo'.

Speke wrote in his *Journal* that the Hindus opened the trade in slaves and ivory possibly some time before the birth of Christ 'with the people of the country of the moon'. But this cannot be true because there is no slavery in the Hindu concept of society. There was no need for slaves, since the Hindu caste system with its distinct divisions of labour took care of all aspects of the job market. Burton wrote about the humanitarian attitude of the Indians of Zanzibar:

> With characteristic tenderness the banyans cook grain at the landing places of slaves, half starved in the middle passage. And inclination as well as policy everywhere induces them to give alms largely.

Apart from Indians financing the slave trade the part they played was no more than that played by British, American, German and French traders who came to the court of Seyyid Said during the 19th century. (Hill, 1949).

British influence over the Indians increased under the guise of restricting British Indian involvement in the slave trade. In 1822 Seyyid Said signed a Treaty with the British whereby he agreed to apprehend British subjects involved in the slave trade. But they were never directly involved, so in this Seyyid Said was not deterred by the various measures the British appeared to take against the trade.

The Industrial Revolution of the late 18th and early19th centuries by its very concept should have eliminated primitive forms of production and chief among them should have been the abolition of slavery. But ironically with Europe's Industrial Revolution the slave trade increased. The trade was being utilized to bring the capitalist mode of production into a primitive area. A new type of market was being created as a result of manufactured goods entering the East African area - consumerism. What was happening in African societies at this stage was that the wants of the people in the African interior were becoming needs and these needs were being met by continuing the slave trade.

For the Indians in general trade with European countries did not work out so well. Europe's Industrial Revolution funded by trade with their colonies in East Africa and India worked adversely for the population. In Africa the slave trade increased, Chiefs who supplied the 'merchandise' became greedy and whereas in the past only prisoners of war were sold as slaves, now peaceful villages were raided to supply men, women and even children to the trade. In India too, peasant farmers were coerced into producing cheap raw materials for the industries in Europe, sometimes at the expense of food crops.

British imperialism saw great potential for controlling the East African markets but this could not be done without the cooperation of the Indian merchants and their capital. Of crucial importance to the British were the well consolidated agencies of the Indian merchants through which British manufactured goods could be distributed throughout the East African region.

> The only State from which any progress or stability can be hoped for is Zanzibar. Its population possesses valuable elements for commerce in the wealthy and numerous settlers from India. (Rigby).

Britain had to be seen to be doing something about abolishing the slave trade, hence it formulated the 1822 Morseby Treaty which brought pressure on Seyyid Said to limit the range of the trade carried on by his subjects. Seyyid Said declared that he was willing to abandon the 'external' trade with foreign states and in particular the sale of slaves to Christians, provided the Treaty would not affect the 'internal' trade in his dominions. The southern Arabs on the East African coast continued to sell slaves to the French and Portuguese since they did not come under the jurisdiction of the British.

The area covered by the Morseby Treaty did not include East Africa to Arabia, and those areas north of Diu (Cutch, Kathiawar) and Oman. In other words the Triangular Trade markets. That is, markets on the west coast of India, east coast of Africa and Oman in Arabia, were being kept open. It is through the Triangular Trade area that Britain intended ultimately to gain control over all the markets in that trade, and the Indian merchant class would play a crucial role in its advancement, because the marketing of British manufactured goods was within these areas. Thus the slave trade as a commercial activity was allowed to continue and the 1833 Act abolishing slavery throughout the British Empire was not intended to cover India, Ceylon (Sri Lanka) or St. Helena.

William Chaplin, Commissioner of the Deccan in Central India expressed this idea clearly:

> Policy and humanity dictate that slavery at some future time shall entirely be prohibited, but all at once to stop the purchase or sale would be equivalent to destruction of what has always been deemed a remarkable commodity and would be at variance with the spirit of the rule which is to follow the usages of the country.

It was apparent to Britain that there should be a definite movement towards a very gradual reduction of the slave trade. It could not be destroyed all at once, but as it was being reduced capital markets would develop to replace it. That was the plan.

On his appointment as the British Consul to Zanzibar one of Hamerton's duties was to work towards the abolition of the slave trade, but he did not seem to be doing anything about it. British imperialism at a certain stage had a vested interest in continuing the trade. The Industrial Revolution was dependent on cheap raw materials from Britain's colonies and the prosperity of the Lancashire Cotton Mills was dependent on slave labour in those colonies. A great part of the wealth which went to build the prosperity of Lancashire at the end of the 18th century which made possible the Industrial Revolution, was derived from the slave trade and the trade from the West Indies linked to it.

The interaction between the Industrial Revolution and the slave trade was of significant importance in the introduction of capitalism into the interior of Africa in the form of manufactured goods from Britain, Europe and America. America used the slave trade to produce goods and services, while Europe used it to sell their manufactured goods, to procure slaves.

Seyyid Said was able to see the connection between manufactured goods and the slave trade. In his instructions to his Envoy to Queen Victoria he stated:

> Now if slaves may be prohibited the whole of the inhabitants of the country will be injured and the revenue will entirely disappear. Firstly they bring revenue from Quiloa (Kilwa) and the coast - ivory and slaves brought together - so that if you prohibit people from coming down and selling slaves you will prohibit them from coming down and selling ivory. Secondly beads from India. If the bringing down of ivory and the dealing in slaves be forbidden, beads will not come. Thirdly, they (people) come from Oman and the Upper country in this way, most of them will cease to come and there will no longer remain purchasers for the goods that come from Europe such as cotton cloth . . .

The logic of this argument could not have failed to impress Britain.

Commenting on Britain's inability to rush into total abolition of slavery Coupland observed:

> Too hasty an attempt therefore to compel Seyyid Said to suppress the trade would be futile and dangerous. He would be compelled to resist it; friendly relations would no longer be possible; the whole situation in the Persian Gulf would be hostile.

Often enough in the course of their long crusade, Britain was compelled to accommodate humanitarian zeal to the exigencies of international relations. This then was the principal motive compelling Britain 'coming to terms' with the slave trade. The other reason was Arab dependence on slave labour in their clove plantations, which in fact was connected with Britain's economic interests.

The Sultan's plea could not be ignored, neither could the Indian merchant class. The capital necessary for clove production came from the Indian merchants to whom the Arabs soon became indebted. In 1841 Capt. Hamerton, the first British Consul observed that Arab clove plantations both in Zanzibar and Pemba were mortgaged to Indian merchants. Three hundred Indian merchants in Pemba controlled the economy of the island. The British needed the Arab ruling class as their political allies and the

Indian merchants as their economic allies, who could purchase the bulk of the manufactured goods and move them into the interior through the network of the slave trade.

And so it was with both the Governments, in Calcutta and Bombay. Policy perforce came first and philanthropy came second. Britain constantly vacillated in suppressing the slave trade. British officials blocked, postponed, diluted and delayed efforts towards what they thought too rapid or too rigorous, actions against slavery. All the same it was quite clear to Britain that there should be a definite move towards a gradual reduction of the slave trade. So even though Britain was not serious about ending the trade immediately, they promulgated the 1845 Hamerton Treaty prohibiting the export of slaves from Seyyid Said's Africa dominions to his Asia dominions.
Burton commented on the reluctance to crush the Slave Trade:

> The Anglo-Indian Government did not in this matter rival the zeal of the home authorities. It lacked earnestness, judging slavery leniently and finding the practice conducive to its subjects.

The British Indian merchants realized the protection given them by British Consul Hamerton, but by no means was this done because of 'finding the practice conducive' to them. Sir Charles Eliot was disturbed that British rule founded to suppress slavery nevertheless maintained and tolerated it in the dominions of the Zanzibar Sultanate. Sir Bartle Frere also observed the vacillation in suppressing the slave trade.

> Our Government representing public opinion appears to me of late years to be very half-hearted in the matter …

Britain's interest was in the raw materials, the import/export trade and control of markets in the entire Triangular Trade area, and this policy ensured the survival of the slave trade in the short term.

In 1872 Lord Granville asked Sir Bartle Frere to make a journey to Zanzibar to negotiate with the Sultan the removal of the slave trade. He was joined by Sir Clement Hill of the Foreign Office, Mr. Charles Grey of the India Office, Dr. Dadger, Arabic scholar and Kazi Shahabudin,

Minister of the Rao (Ruler) of Cutch. The Minister represented the Indians who were subjects of the Rao through whom all the trade on the East African coast was carried out. Kazi Shahabuddin, Dewar of Cutch proved most helpful. He appealed to the Indians in the name of the Maharao of Cutch to abstain from any dealings in slavery and warned that if they did not stop, their property in Cutch would be confiscated. Even though they lost millions of dollars the Indians readily agreed and freed all their slaves.

The time when the Slave Trade was crushed was also the time when merchant capital dominated the East African economy. Thenceforth Indian merchant capital had no independent existence. Indian merchants had a big stake in the East African economy, they possessed half the landed property in Zanzibar and a large amount of money invested in East Africa. Indian merchant capital was trapped to serve the new mode, the capitalist mode of production, which they were forced to accept in order to maintain some semblance of independence (Sakarai, 1981).

From the 17th to the end of the 18th centuries British shipping touched at the Comoros Isles and passed directly on to India carrying British manufactured goods. These goods then entered the East African market as British Indian goods. Thus by deliberate design Britain kept her shipping away from Zanzibar while America, Germany, Portugal, Prussia, Spain, Denmark, Hanover and France were left to compete for the Zanzibar markets. American and German merchants were driving the French out of Zanzibar. From 1855 to 1859 it was noted that 154 American and 97 Hamburg ships called at Zanzibar as compared with only two British. The British were occupied with consolidating their position in the largest markets in the Indian Ocean - the Indian markets! British goods entered the East African market through the west coast of India which was the commercial base of the Indian merchants, and seized the Triangular Trade. By the 1860s British trade with Zanzibar through their British Indian subjects, began to exceed that of all other countries.

When Britain was assured of control over the entire area of the Triangular Trade, she set about ruthlessly suppressing the slave trade at its source - the Chiefs. One of the slave trading Chiefs, Mlozi of North Nyasa was hanged and another, Chief Mwasi, who closed the trade routes from Nyasa to Congo was subdued. By 1893 the slave trade was abolished in the Sultan's mainland possessions and by 1907 the trade was effectively abolished.

Chapter 17

Plants introduced into Africa from Asia

The most significant impact of trade with ancient Azania on world history was the introduction of plants from Asia. The first cultivated plants of Indian origin reached East Africa via the Sabean Lane, some of which were introduced into north Africa (Ethiopia). Later, merchant vessels travelling with the Monsoons in either direction loaded up with supplies that were available, with the result that the coasts of Azania and western India came to share the same roster of food crops. This was thought to have happened in the first millennium BC. But archeological work in Africa and historical research in India put the date further back in time. (Chattopadhyaya, 1970).

> Madagascar was settled by peoples of Indonesia about BC 2,000. They brought rice and bananas to Africa which became an important staple in the Bantu diet. About the same time India introduced on the East African coast crops which became important to Swahili culture. Sugarcane, coconuts, Asian rice, root plants, and lentils. Sugarcane was introduced from India into Kenya, Uganda and Mauritius. (Curtin, 1978).

The Hindus were trading with East Africa as early as the 6th century BC, almost certainly it was they who introduced the coconut palm to Africa. (Coupland, 1938).

A white historian writing in 1595 said that in the Great Lakes Region there were busy markets, and a French missionary wrote that the Bakongo grew oranges, lemons, guavas, and other small fruits unknown to Europeans. These fruits could only have come with the Indians who entered Africa through the north.

> Between the islands of Sao Lorenço (Madagascar) and the mainland are three islands. The Comoros Isles, inhabited by Moors which have great store of food. Rice, oranges, limes, citrons, sugarcane and every kind of fruit. (Barbosa, 1502).

In 1906, 1,000 acres were allotted to Indians in Kibos and Kisumu in Nyanza Province. This fertile land produced maize, sugarcane, cotton and chillies. (Kotecha, 1994) all introduced from India. Near the Lake in Kavirondo cotton was grown by Indians. Indian cultivators excelled in the growing of the cotton crop which became an important export article (Chattophadyaya, 1970). The farms in and around Muhoroni were owned and cultivated by Indians which became the most important sugar producing areas in Kenya. Indians were also given thousands of acres of land that was semi-arid and stony in the Machakos district. But with irrigation the land produced quality fruit and Indian vegetables. (Ferrant, 1981).

Many plants recur in Africa and India such as millets *(sorghum valgare*), simsim (*sesamum orientale*) and pulses, the number, variety and concentration in the interior of Africa could not be recent. Cotton grown in Sudan and Ethiopia belong to two species. The *Gossypium arboretum* variety is known to have been woven in *Mohen-jo-daro* in the 3rd millennium BC. (McEwan, 1968).

On Da Gama's second voyage in 1502 he stopped at Zanzibar, the green island. The harbour was full of dhows engaged in trade. Gardens and orchards thick with vegetables and fruit, oranges, limes, mangoes and all types of tropical fruit and vegetables. Pemba, Mafia and Zanzibar lying within the Kilwa sphere of influence produced sugarcane and citrus fruits. Malindi had rich orchards, fields of wheat, rice and millet. According to Barbosa, the Indians took from India to Mombasa round tail sheep, cows, fowls, much millet, rice, sweet and bitter oranges, lemons and pomegranates, Indian figs and Indian vegetables.

Dr. Livingstone was struck by the mutual trade carried on between

India and Africa when he travelled in India. He realized that there was unlimited capacity to produce food in Africa. Grain which suited the Indian taste was produced a little distance from the coast, particularly the coast around Mombasa. In times of famine in India food grain was imported from Africa.

A few of the horticultural products introduced into Africa from Asia listed below:

Trees

coconut palm	mango
jackfruit	tamarind
guava	cashew

Grains

millet	sorghum
rice	simsim
wheat	sesame

Fruit

sweet and bitter oranges	Indian figs
limes	bananas (from Malaysia)
lemons	pomegranates
grapefruit	pineapples
papaya	

Vegetables and legumes

Okra	sweet potatoes	gram bean or mung bean
egg plant or brinjal	cow peas	hyacinth bean or lab lab bean
ground nuts	chillies	pigeon pea
cucumber.		

Root plants	**Medicinal**	**Cash crops**
ginger	camphor	sugarcane
garlic	neem	cotton
onions (Goa)	tulsi	rice

These are the most important crops and of course spices: cumin, corrianda, pepper, tumeric, mustard, fenegruk, cardamom, cinnamon.

Chapter 18

Globalization by Trade

For all the importance of local commerce it was international trade that created the wealth that brought Eastern Africa to the orbit of the world economy.
(Malyn Newitt in A *History of Mozambique*, 1995)

Indians imported goods from all over the world. The advertisements included products available from countries as far away as Europe, America and Japan. Listed below are some of the major and minor Indian trading firms.

Cowasjee Dinshaw & Bros.
The name is a household word on the East African Coast
Firm Estd. in 1884 in Zanzibar and in Aden 70 years ago.
Head Office in Aden
Aden, Bombay, Zanzibar, Djibouti, Benadir & Somalia Coasts
Bankers & General Merchants
H.M.S. Naval and Military Contractors
Importers of Wines, spirits & piece goods from England & USA
Shipping and general merchants
Shipowners, steamers stopping during Monsoons

Agents for: British Tanganyika Territory Government
Oriental Government Security Life Insurance Co. Ltd.

Thomas Cook & Sons
Clearing & Forwarding Agents
United Exporters

New India Assurance Co.

Tokio Marine & Fire Insurance Co.

Abdulhusein Gulamhusein & Bros.
Distributor for Zanzibar Protectorate
Use American Solpet Brand & Kerosene - the best
Crysler Corporation, Export Division
Detroit (Michigan)

Yoosufali Nurbhai Pishori
Headquarters in Zanzibar
Established in 1884
Imports coming from Karachi

Fazal H. Nassar
Merchants & Commission Agents
Importers & Exporters - Zanzibar
Agencies throughout Kenya & Tanganyika
Branches in Belgium & French Congo

Merchant Bank of Zanzibar
Messers. Virchand Panachand & Co.
Nairobi Agent: Mulji Jetha, Banker

Huseinali Dharamshi Hasmani
Hercules Cycle & Motor Co.
Anything you require from Japan
Just drop few lines for what you want

Juduvji Dewji
Best known as importers of lace

Walji Heerji & Bros.
Established more than 20 years ago as
General Merchants and Commission Agents
Importers and Exporters. Have a branch in Nairobi
Imports mainly Rubber

Mohamed Dhunjee
For a number of years he has been established in Mombasa as a Clearing & Forwarding & Commission Agent
Large quantities of lamps, glass and earthenware are imported from England

B. Singho Appu
Manufacturing Jeweller who is prepared to undertake the processing or mounting of all kinds of oriental gems or curio
Chinese and Japanese silverware and fancy goods and Ceylonese and Maltese Lace

Bundaly Hirjee & Co.
In Zanzibar for a quarter of a century
Grain & Rice Importers - exporters of cloves, copra

Karimjee Jivanjee & Co. Zanzibar
Established in Zanzibar in 1840 as general Import & Export merchants
Mombasa, Dar es Salaam, Tanga, Lindi, Makindani
Sole agents for Italian Olive Oil
Ironwood screws, hinges etc.
English biscuits
Links with Italy, Sheffield, India, New York, Leipzig, Genoa

Kassamali Ismail & Co.
Reliable Indenting (Requisitioning) House
Zanzibar, Tanga, Dar es Salaam

Esmailjee Jivanjee & Co.
Founded in Zanzibar in 1819 by Mr. Jivanjee Budhabhoy of Cutch Mandvi (Then known by his name)
Present Firm estd. 1925
Mombasa, Dar es Salaam, Tanga, Lindi, Makindani
The Directors are H.E. Jivanjee & Y.E. Jivanjee, natives of Cutch Mandvi in India
There are few roads in Zanzibar and Mombasa where the enterprising firm is not respected
Mill & Estate Owners & General Import & Export Merchants

Lands, Estates, 2,000 acres in British East Africa
Extract oils from custard seeds, coconuts & sim sim
Soap, rice, flour, machineries
Have founded Electric Light & Power Co.
Big stores of hardware in Mombasa & Zanzibar
Import - Manchester cotton goods; sugar from Austria; rice from India, tea, coffee
Export - cloves, copra, hides, beeswax, rubber, chillies, and groundnuts
Certificate of Merit for cloves in Zanzibar 1905
Ship direct to: Europe, India, Ceylon. From East African ports, Lamu, Malindi,
Seychelles, Madagascar
Have many dhows

Business, then as now was risk taking. Many did not make it and had to be content to work for other traders, perhaps all of their lives:

> The notion that procuring, pricing and distributing goods was all there is to it, or that communal relations protected the shopkeeper, is off the mark. A fierce competition that kept the traders occupied from dawn to dusk and their profit margins small, also existed . . . in Asian enterprises. After meeting the cost of living, their directors put everything back into the businesses and when possible went into industry. (Seidenberg, 1996).

None of the business establishments still exist in their original form. Some have closed down but most have moved from the 'primary products' sector into the 'secondary producing and manufacturing' sector. In 'promoting the production sector' the most spectacular example is the Chandaria family. Originally farmers in Jamnagar, they are foremost among the Indians now moved into the 'import-substitution sector.' (Seidenberg, 1996).

In *The Success story of Indians from East Africa* Vinod Raja cites the success story of several former East African residents, mainly from Uganda and Kenya. The Uganda Indians were expelled by Idi Amin in 1972, notably Manubhai Madhivani and his family, and other 'sugar barons' because they controlled about 12% of the national economy. Some of the family has now returned to Uganda, where they again control 'a huge swathe of the economy.' The Jatanias are another ex-Ugandan family who migrated to London in 1969. They made their fortune acquiring poorly performing consumer brands and 'turning them around'. Shailesh Vara, a former vice-president of Britain's Conservative Party, is now a Conservative Member of Parliament. Tarique Ghaffur, is now Assistant Commissioner of London's Metropolitan Police. Both Indians were born in Uganda.

Jasmindar Singh went to Britain from Kenya. He has made his £350 million fortune from hotels. His family owns the prestigious Raddisson Edwardian hotel chain. Jasmindar a former St. Theresa Boys' School student, offered one of his hotels for the reunion of students of his former school in 2005 in Britain. This is just one Kenyan family that made a fortune more recently.

There is the Pathak family. They arrived in Britain from Kenya in the 1950s and made a living selling food to the local Indian community. That helped them win a contract to supply food to Ugandan Indians in British refugee camps in the early 1970s. From this small beginning Pathak's Original brand of curry sauces, chutneys and pickles was born. These products are sold around the world and the family is now worth about £60 million.

If one goes back and examines the roots of all the rich Indian families now living in East Africa and those who have made their home in other parts of the world one might find that the origin of their wealth was in the distant past as humble dukawallahs in East Africa and elsewhere. There are also those like Lakshmi Mittal whose bid for the multibillion dollar second-biggest steel producer, Arcelor, cannot be without sound foundation.

It is rumoured that in many countries where Indians have settled including Kenya, the community pays the highest taxes.

References

a Huan (1970). The Overall Survey of the Ocean's Shores. J. V. G. Mills, trans. Cambridge.

Abramson, H. J. Migrants and Cultural Diversity: On Ethnicity and Religion. *In Social Compass*, vol. No. 1, pp. 5-29.

Aduboahen, A. Ed. (1990). Africa Under Colonial Domination 1880-1935. In General *History of Africa,* Vol. VII, California.

Afigbo, A. E. et al. Eds. (1968). *The Making of Modern Africa.* Essex, England, Longman.

Africa and the Indian Ocean in Chinese Maps of the Fourteenth and Fifteenth Centuries. In *Imago Mundi*, vol. 24, 1970.

Afro-Shirazi Party. Executive Dept. & Education Dept. (1974). *A Short History of Zanzibar.*

Ahluwalia, M. M. *Indian History and Culture* (1993). New Delhi: Golgotia Publications.

Ahmad, Afzal. *Indian Textiles and the Portuguese Trade in the 17th Century* (1600-1663). *See Stvdia*

al-Mas'udi *Les prairies d'or* (1861-77). C. B. Meynard and P. de Courtielle, Eds. and trans.

Albuquerque, A. Commentaries of Alfonse de Albuquerque (1875-1884). W. G. de Birch, trans. 4 vols.

Alder, G. J. *Britain and the Defense of India: The Origins of the problems, 1798-1815.* (1972). *In Journal of African History*, vol. 6.

Ali, S. M. *The Geography of the Puranas.* (1966). New Delhi.

Allen, J. de V. The *East African Slave Trade.* (1985). Nairobi: East African Publishing House. In *Historical Association of Tanzania,* Paper No. 3.

Allen, J. de V. Habash, Habish, Sidi, Sayyid. (1985). In, J. C. Stone, Ed. *Africa and the Sea.* Aberdeen.

Alpers, E. *A Gujerat and the Trade of East Africa.* (1976). In *African Historical Studies,* vol. 9, Boston.

Alpers, Edward A. *The East African Slave Trade.* (1967). Nairobi: East African Publishing House.

Alpers, Edward A. *Gujerat and the trade of East Africa, 1500-1800.* (1976). In *International Journal of African Historical Studies.* California: University of California Press.

Alpers, Edward A. *Ivory and Slaves in East Central Africa: Changing Patterns of International Trade to the Later Nineteenth Century.* (1975), London, Heinemann.

Altrincham, Lord. (Formerly Sir Edward Grigg, Governor of Kenya, 1925-1931). *Kenya's Opportunity, Memories, Hopes and Ideas.* London: Faber and Faber Limited.

Amier, Haji Amier. *The Rule of the Mwenye Mkuu of Unguja.* (1992). International Conference on the History and Culture of Zanzibar, December 14-16, 1992.

Anderson, John. *The Struggle for the School.* (1970). Nairobi, Longman Kenya.

Annual Report of the East Africa Indian National Congress for the year 1923, 16th and 17th Sept. 1922. Chairman, Malkiat Singh. Report on the 'Indian Question'.
Atieno-Odhiambo, E. S. *The Political Economy of the Asian Problem in Kenya., 1888-1938.* (1974). In *Transafrican Journal of History*, vol. 4, nos. 1 & 2.

Aubin, Jean (1988). See Lombard, D.

Axel,E. *Portuguese in South East Africa, 1488-1600.* (1930). Cape Town.

Axel, E. *Portuguese in South East Africa, 1600-1799.* (1960). Johannesburg.

Ayrout, Henry Habib. *Liaisons Africaines.* (1975). Le Caire: S.O.P. Press.

Azania: Journal of the British Institute of History and Archeology in Nairobi. London: Oxford University Press, 1961.

Babajee, Esnoo. *Mauritian Affairs.* (1957). Bombay: Hind Kitab Ltd.

Bakari, Mohamed. *Asian Muslims in Kenya.* (1999). Nairobi: Mewa Publications.

Banaji, D. R. *Slavery in British India.* (1933). Bombay.

Barbosa, Duarte. *The Book of Duarte Barbosa,* vol. I (1918). Translated from the Portuguese text by Marcel Longworth Dames. London: Printed for the Haklyut Society.

Barbosa, Duarte. *An Account of the East Coast c1517-18.* (1908). Translated from the *Book of Duarte Barbosa,* vol. I, pp. 6-29. Edited by M. L. Dames for Haklyut Society.

Bawra, Brahmvisho Vishvatma. *The Hindu Way of Life.* I. C. Sharma and Brahmita, trans. Chandigarh: Divyalok Prakashan.

Beachey, R. W. A Collection of Documents on the Slave Trade of Eastern Africa. (1976). London, Collings.

Beachey, R. W. *The Slave Trade of Eastern Africa.* (1976). New York, Barnes and Noble.

Benedetto, L. F. and Ricci, A. trans. *The Travels of Marco Polo.* (1931), London.

Bennet, Charles. Persistence and Adversity: *The Growth and spatial distribution of the Asian population in Kenya,* 1902-1963. (1977). Ph.D. Dissertation, Syracuse University.

Bennett, Norman R. (1984). The Arab State of Zanzibar: A Bibliography. Boston, G. K. Hall.

Bennett, Norman R. Ed. *The Zanzibar Letters of Edward D. Ropes, Jr.* (1973). Boston, Boston University Press.

Bennett, N. R. Ed. Stanley's Dispatches to the New York Herald. (1970). Boston.

Bhana, Surendra and Brian, Joy B. *Setting Down Roots: Indian migrants in South Africa, 1860-1911.* (1990). Johannesburg, Witwatersrand University Press.

Bharati, Agehananda. *The Asians in East Africa: Jaihind and Uhuru.* (1972). Professional Series, Chicago, Nelson-Hall Co.

Bhattacharya, D. K. *Indians of African Origin.* (1970). *In Cahiers d'etude africaines,* vol. 40.

Boteler, Capt. Thomas Narrative of a Voyage of Discovery to Africa and Arabia. Performed by Her Majesty's Ships, Levan and Barracuta from 1821 to 1826 under the command of Capt. F.W.Owen, (1935), London.

Boxer, C. R. *From Lisbon to Goa,* 1500-1750, (1984), London. Boxer, C. R. and De Azevedo, C. *The Portuguese in Mombasa,* (1960), London.

Brady, Cyrus Townsend. *Commerce and Conquest in East Africa,* with Particular Reference to the Salem Trade with Zanzibar . (1950). Salem, Essex Institute.

Bridges, R. C. *The Historical Role of British Explorers in East Africa.* (1982). *In Terrae Incognital,* no. 14.

Bridges, R. C. James. Augustus Grant's Visual Record of East Africa. Annual Lecture to the Hakluyt Society.

Bridges, R. C. Nineteenth Century East African Travel Records. (1977). In *Paideuma*, no. 33.

British East Africa Indian Congress. Presidential Address by Mr. A. M. Jeevanjee, 1st Session, 1914. Racial Prejudice in the Legislature between European and Indian settlers. 3rd Session, 1920. Future trouble.

British East Africa Indian Congress. Later became the East Africa Indian National Congress.

British East Africa Miscellaneous Papers. The Murumbi Collection.

British Empire of India (The), (1905), Vol. III, Economic, in *The Imperial Gazeteer of India*. Oxford, Clarendon Press.

Buddenhagen, I. W. and Persley, G. J. Eds. Rice in Africa, London.

Bujadluer, Aunauth. *Indians in Mauritius.* (1995). Quatre Bornes: Pandit Ramlakhan Gossange Publication.

Burnstein, F. M. *The Erythrean Sea.* (1989). Cambridge.

Burton, Richard F. (1872).The Hindoos of Zanzibar and East Africa. Extract from *Zanzibar*. London, Tinsley Brothers.

Burton, R. F.The *Lake Regions of Central Africa.* (1860), London.

Burton, R. F. *Zanzibar: City, Island and Coast.* (1872). London, Tinsley Brothers.

Burwash, D. English Merchant Shipping, 1450-1540, (1974), Toronto.

Calpin, G. H. C. *Indians in South Africa,* (1949), Pietermaritzburg, Shutter and Shooter.

Carpenter, A. J. *The History of Rice in Africa,* (1979), London.

Cassen, L. *Ships and Steamships in the Ancient World,* (1971), Princeton.

Centenary Celebrations Brochure (1998), Nairobi, St. Austin's Parish.

Chandra, Satish Ed. *The Indian Ocean Explorers*, (1987). *In History Commerce and Politics.* New Delhi, Sage Publications.

Chatopadyaya, Haraprasad. *Indians in Africa*: *A Socio-economic Study*, (1970). Calcutta, Bookland Private Ltd.

Chaudhuri, K. N. and Manoharlal, Munshiram. *Trade and Civilization in the Indian Ocean: An Economic history from the rise of Islam to 1570.* (1985). Delhi, Munshiram Publications.

Chinweizu. *The West and the Rest of Us.* (1975). New York, Vantage Books.

Chittick, H. Neville and Rotberg, Robert I., Eds. *East Africa and the Orient: Cultural synthesis in pre-colonial times.* (1975), New York, African Publishing Co.

Chittick, N. *Kilwa, an Islamic Trading City on the East African Coast*, (1989), 2 vols, Nairobi.

Chronicles of the Indian Societies in Zanzibar.

Churchill,Winston, S. *My African Journey*, (1908), London.

Cipolla, C. M. *Guns and Sails in the Early Phase of European Expansion,* 1400-1700, (1965), London.

Clarence-Smith, W. G. *The Economics of the Indian Ocean Slave Trade in the Nineteenth Century*, (1989), London, England. Ottawa, N.J., Frank Cass.

Collins, Robert O. Ed. *African History*, (1971), Santa Barbara, University of California.

Collins, Robert O. *Eastern African History*, New York, M. Wiener Publishing.

Collins, Robert O. *Europe in Africa*, (1993), New York, Alfred Knof.

Collister, Peter. *The Last Days of Slavery: England and the East African Slave Trade, 1870-1900.* (1969), Dar es Salaam, East African Literature Bureau.

Colomb, Philip Howard. *Slave-catching in the Indian Ocean: A Record of naval experiences*. Reprint of 1873 ed. New York, Negro Universities Press. Commissariat, M. S. *History of Gujerat,* (1938), Bombay.

Condiffe, J. B. The Commerce of Nations, (1951), London.

Correa, G. *The Three Voyages of Vasco da Gama*, (1869), H. E. J. Stanley, trans. from *Lendes da India*, London.

Correa-Alfonso, Ahmad Ibn-Majid and the Sea Route to India. (1964). In Indica, September 1964, no. 2, Bombay, Heras Institute of Indian History and Culture.

Coupland, Reginald. *East Africa and its Invaders*. (1969), New York, Russel & Russel.

Coupland, Reginald. *East Africa and Its Invaders: From Earliest times to the death of Seyyid Said in 1856*, (1938), Oxford, The Clarendon Press.

Coupland, Reginald. *The Exploitation of East Africa, 1856-1890: The Slave Trade and The Scramble,* (1939), London, Faber and Faber.

Coupland, Reginald. *The Exploitation of East Africa, 1856-1890: The Slave Trade and The Scramble*, 2nd ed. London, Faber and Faber.

Crawford, O. G. S. *Some Medieval Theories about the Nile*. (1949), London.

Crofton, H. R. (1936). *A Pageant of Spice Islands*. London.

Crowder, Michael. *White Chiefs of Africa. In Colonialism in Africa*, 1960-1970.

Curtin, Philip, et al. *African History*, (1978), London, Longman.

Curtin, Philip, et al. *African History from Earliest Times to Independence,* (1995), 2nd ed, NewYork.

Dale, Godfrey. *The Peoples of Zanzibar*, (1920), New York, Negro Universities Press.

Dames, M. L. *The Portuguese and Turks in the Indian Ocean in the Sixteenth Century*. In JRAS.

Danvers, F. C. *The Portuguese in India*, (1894), London.

Das, P. K. *The Monsoons,* (1968), London.

Davidson, Basil. *Africa: History of a Continent*, (1966), London, Spring Books.

Davidson, Basil. *Africa in History*. (1964). New York, The Macmillan Co.

Davidson, Basil. *African Kingdoms*. (1967). A History of the World. Series: Great Ages of Man. Nederlands: Time-Life International.

Davidson, Basil. *The African Past: Chronicles from antiquity to modern times*, (1964), London, Longman.

Davidson, Basil. *Discovering Africa's Past*, (1978), Harlow, Longman Group.

Davidson, Basil. *East and Central Africa to the Late Nineteenth Century*, (1967), London, Longmans.

Davidson, Basil. *A History of East and Central Africa to the Late Nineteenth century*. Garden City, (1959), New York, Anchor Books.

Davidson, Basil (1959). *The Lost Cities of Africa*. Boston: Little Brown & Co.

Davidson, Basil. *Old Africa Rediscovered,* (1959), London, Victor Gollanez.

Davidson, C. and Clark, J. D. *Trade Wind Beads,* (1974), In Azania, vol. 9.

Dawood, N. J. Ed. *Tales from the Thousand and One Nights,* (1973), London.

Deerpalsingh, Saloni and Carter, Marina. Select Documents on Indian Immigration, Mauritius 1834-1926. Vol III, *Living and Working Conditions Under Indenture.* Moka, Mahatma Gandhi Institute.

Delf, George. *The Asians in East Africa,* (1963), London.

Denham, E. B. *Ceylon Census Returns,* (1912), Colombo.

Depelchin, Jacques. *The Transition from Slavery, 1873-1914.* (1991). *In Zanzibar Under Colonial Rule,* Sheriff, Abdul and Ferguson, Ed. Eds. London: James Curry.

Deschamps, H. *Histoire de Madagascar,* (1960), Paris.

Deschamps, H. Les pirates a Madagascar, (1949), Paris.

Dilley, Marjorie Ruth. *British Policy in Kenya Colony.* (1966). New York, Barnes & Noble.

Dotson, Floyd and Dotson, Lillian O. *The Indian Minority of Zambia, Rhodesia and Malawi,* (1968), New Haven,Yale University Press.

Duffy, J. *Portugal in Africa.* (1962), London.

Duffy, James. *Portuguese in Africa.* (1959), Cambridge, Massachusetts: Harvard University Press.

Dunn, R. E. *The Adventures of Ibn Battuta,* (1986), Berkley.

Duyvendak, J. J. L. *China's Discovery of Africa,* (1949), London.

Earl of Lytton. See Lytton, Noel Anthony.

East Africa Indian National Congress. (Later became the Kenya Indian National Congress.) Presidential Address by Mr. A. M. Jeevanjee. 3rd series 1920. "I hate the so-called patience of the Indian . . . "
East Africa Indian National Congress. Annual Report for the Year 1923, 16th and 17th September 1923. On the Indian Question.

East Africa Indian National Congress. Indian Settlement in Kenya. Presidential Address by By Mr. Tayeb Ali 1927. "The first British Consulate was opened in Zanzibar to protect the interests of their Indian subjects who were already there long before the British had heard about Africa."

East Africa Indian National Congress held in Mombasa 25th-26th December, 1934. Address by K. K. Pradhan, Chairman, 13th Session. Indian Emigration to East Africa.

East Africa Indian National Congress, 13th Session, 25-26 Dec.1934. Address by Mr. K. K. Pradhan, Chairman. "White Settlement had not been self-sufficient . . ."

East Africa Today, 1958-1959. A Comprehensive Directory of British East Africa with Who's Who. Vaghella, B. B. Ed. Bombay: Overseas Information Publishers.

Eliot, Charles, Sir. The East African Protectorate, (1905), London: Edward Arnold.

Encyclopedia Americana. (1958), New York: Americana Corporation.

Fage, J. D. *A History of Africa,* (1978), London.

Ferrant, Leda. *The Legendary Grogan: The Only man to trek from Cape to Cairo: Kenya's controversial pioneer,* (1981), London: Hanish Hamilton.

Ferrant, Leda. *Tippu Tip and the East African Slave Trade*, (1979), London: Hamilton.

Ferguson, Ed and Shariff, Abdul, Eds. *The Formation of a Colonial Economy*, (1991). In *Zanzibar Under Colonial Rule*. London: James Curry.

Filesi, T. *China and Africa in the Middle Ages*, (1972), London.

Foran, W. Robert. *The Kenya Police (1887-1960), (1962)*, London: Robert Hale Ltd.

Fordham, Paul. *The Geography of African Affairs*, (1964), Harmondsworth, Middlesex, England: Penguin Books Ltd.

Forest, G. W. Ed. Travels and Journals, (1906), Preserved in the Bombay Secretariat, Bombay.

Frazler, Franklin E. *Race Relations, Culture Contacts in the Modern World*, (1906), Boston, Beacon Press.

Freeman-Grenville, G. S. P. *The East African Coast: Select documents from the first to the earlier nineteenth century*, (1962), Oxford: Clarendon Press.

Freeman-Grenville, G. S. P. (1975). *The East African Coast: Selected Documents from the first to the earlier nineteenth century*, 2nd ed. London: Collings.

Freeman-Grenville, G. S. P. *Historiography of the East African Coast*: A Paper presented to the historians and archivist of the Indian Ocean, (1960).Tananarive, Madagascar.

Freeman-Grenville, G. S. P. *The Industrial History of the Coast of Tanganyika with Special Reference to Recent Archaeological Discoveries*, (1962). London: Oxford University Press.

Freeman-Grenville, G. S. P. Ed. The, *Mombasa Rising Against the Portuguese 1631 from Sworn Evidence*, London: Oxford University Press for the British Academy.

Freeman-Grenville, G. S. P. *The Portuguese on the Swahili Coast: Buildings and language*, London.

Freund, Bill. *The Making of Contemporary Africa*, (1990), Boulder, Colorado, Lynne Rienner Publishers.

Gadre, Medha Vishwas. *India's Cultural Links with Africa since Ancient Times*. In Afro-Hindu Vision

Gailey, Harry A. Jr. *History of Africa since Earliest Times to 1800*, (1970), New York, Holt, Rinehart and Winston Inc.

Gailey, Harry A. Jr. *History of Africa from 1800 to the Present*, (1972), New York, Holt, Rinehart and Winston Inc.

Galbraith, John S. *Mackinnon and East Africa*, 1878-1895: *A Study in The New Imperialism*. (1972), Cambridge, England, University Press.

Gangulee, N. *Indians in the Empire Overseas*, (1947), London.

Gann, I. H. and Duigan, Peter, Eds. *Colonialism in Africa*, 1870-1960, (1970), London, Cambridge University Press.

Gann, I. H. & Duigan, Peter. *The Rulers of British Africa, 1870-1914*, (1987), London, Croom Helm.

Gann, Iweis H. and Duigan, Peter. *White Settlers in Tropical Africa*, (1962), Baltimore, Penguin Books.

Gann, Iweis H. and Duigan, Peter. *White Settlers in Tropical Africa*, (1977), Westport, Conn., Greenwood Press.

Garlake, P. *Great Zimbabwe*, (1982), London.

Garlake, P. The *Kingdoms of Africa*, (1978), London.

George, Rosemary. *The Politics of Home: Post colonial relations and twentieth century Fiction*, (1966), Cambridge, Cambridge University Press.

Gervase, P. *Early Islamic Architecture of the East African Coast*, (1978), Oxford.

Gervase, Roland Anthony Oliver Mathew, Ed. *History of East Africa: The Early Period*, (1976), Nairobi, Oxford University Press.

Ghai, Dharam P. and Ghai, Yash P. Eds. *Portrait of a Minority*, (1990), Nairobi, Oxford University Press.

Gillman, C. *Dar es Salaam 1949-1960*, (1945). In *Tanganyika Notes and Records*, No. 20.

Glassman, Jonathan. *Feasts and Riots: Revelry, rebellion and popular consciousness on the Swahili Coast*, 1856-1888, (1955), Portsmouth, NH, Heinemann.

Gordon-Brown, A. Ed. *The South and East African Year Book & Guide: With Atlas, town plans and diagrams*, (1948), London, Samson Low, Marsdon & Co.

Gorinden, Devarakshanam. *Memory is a Weapon: Reading under Apartheid*. (1996), In *Ariel*, 27, 1.

Grandidier, A. et al. Collection des ouvrages ancient concernment Madagascar, (1905), Paris.

Gray, J. *Visit of a French Ship to Kilwa in 1527*, (1964). In *Tanganyika Notes and Records*, no. 63

Gray, J. A. *The British in Mombasa*, (1957), London.

Gray, John, Sir. *History of Zanzibar from the Middle Ages to 1856*, (1962), London, Oxford University Press.

Gray, John. *History of Zanzibar from the Middle Ages to 1856*. (1975). Reprint of 1962 ed. Westport, Conn.,Greenwood Press.

Gray, R. and Birmingham, D. Eds. *Pre-Colonial African Trade*, (1970), Oxford.
Great Britain. British Information Service (1963). Zanzibar: New York: Great Britain Information Service.

Great Britain. Empire Marketing Board. Statistics & Intelligence Branch (1931). Production and Trade of Zanzibar. London: HMSO.

Gregory, Robert G. *India and East Africa: A History of Race Relations within the British Empire, 1890-1939)*, (1971), Oxford, Clarendon Press.

Gregory, Robert G. *Quest for Equality: Asian Politics in East Africa, 1900-1967*, (1993), New Delhi, Orient Longman Ltd.

Grewal, N. S. *Pioneers in East Africa*, (1967), *In Journal of African and Asian Studies*, no. 1, pp. 66-89.

Grey, C. *Pirates of the Eastern Seas*, (1934), London.

Grosset-Grange, H. La Cote africaines dans la routieres nautique arabes au moment des Grandes decouvertes, (1978). In Azania, vol. 13.

Gunawardana, R. A. L. H. *Seaways to Sielediba*. (1958). Paper for Delhi Seminar on the Indian Ocean, Peradeniya, Sri Lanka.

Gunther, John. *Inside Africa*, (1955), London, Hamish Hamilton.

Gupta, Vijay. *Kenya Politics of (In)dependence*, (1981), New Delhi, Peoples Publishing House.

Haight, Mabel V. Jackson. *European Powers and South-East Africa: A Study of international relations on the south-coast of Africa, 1796-1856*. (1967). Rev. ed. London, Routledge & K. Paul.

Hail, M. *The Changing Past: Farmers, kings and traders in South Africa, 1200-1860*, (1987), Cape Town.

Hailey, Lord. *An African Survey: A Survey of Problems arising in Africa South of the Sahara, (1957)*, London, Oxford University Press.

Haines, Grove C. Ed. Africa Today, (1955), Baltimore, Johns Hopkins University Press.

Hall, Richard. *Empires of the Monsoon: A History of the Indian Ocean and its Invaders,* (1998), Hammersmith, London: Harper-Collins.

Hall, Stuart. *Cultural Identity and Diaspora,* (1993). In Patrick Williams and Laura Chrisman Harvester, Eds. *Colonial Discourse and Post-Colonial Theory,* pp. 392-403.

Hallet, Robin. *Africa Since 1875,* (1980), London, Heinemann.

Hamdun, Said and King, Noel. *Ibn Battuta in Black Africa,* (1994), Princeton, M. Weiner Publishers.

Hamiton, Genesta. *In the Wake of da Gama: The Story of Portuguese pioneers in East Africa, 1497-1727,* (1951). With an Introduction by Elspeth Huxley. London, Skeffington and Sons Ltd.

Hamiton, Genesta. *Princes of Zinj: The Rulers of Zanzibar.* (1957), London, Hutchinson.

Hamiton, Genesta. *Princes of Zinj: The Rulers of Zanzibar; of the East African Slave Trade,* (1957), Evanston, Northwestern University Press.

Hamond, W. A. *A Paradox Proving that the People of Madagascar are the Happiest in the World,* (1940), London.

Hamoud al-Maamiry, Ahmed. *Oman and East Africa,* (1979), New Delhi, Lancers Publishers.

Hancock, W. K. *Indians in Kenya,* (1964). In *A Survey of British Comonwealth Affairs,* London, Oxford University Press.

Hardy, Ronald. *The Iron Snake,* (1965), London, St. James Palace.

Harlow, Vincent & Chilvers, E. M. Eds. *History of East Africa,* Vols.I & II. (1965), London, Oxford University Press.

Harris, Joseph E. *The African Presence in Asia: Consequences of the East African Slave Trade,* (1971), Evanston, Northwestern University Press.

Harrison-Church, R. J. Africa and the Islands, (1971), London.

Hart, H. Extracts from brief notes of a visit to Zanzibar in Hart's ship *Imogene,* January and February 1834.

Hazaresingh, K. A. *A History of Indians in Mauritius,* (1950), Port Louis.

Henning, C. G. *The Indentured Indian in Natal,* 1860-1917, (1993), New Delhi, Promilla & Co.

Herskovits, Melville J. *The Human Factor in Changing Africa,* (1958), London, Routledge & Kegan Paul.

Hill, M. F. *Permanent Way: The Story of the Kenya and Uganda Railway,* (1949). 2nd ed. Nairobi, East African Railways and Harbours.

Hinawy, Mbarak Ali. *Al-Akida and Fort Jesus, Mombasa,* (1970), 2nd ed. Nairobi, East African Literature Bureau.

Hirth, F. and Rockhill, W. W. trans. *Chau Ju-Kwa: His Works on the Chinese and Arab trade in the 12th and 13th centuries,* (1911), St. Petersburg.

Historical Relations Across the Indian Ocean: Report and papers of the Meeting of Experts. Organized by UNESCO at Port Louis, Mauritius from 15 to 19 July 1974. Paris: UNESCO, 1980.

Hitti, Phillip K. *History of the Arabs,* (1937). *In Works on the Chinese and Arab Trade in the*

12th Century, London, Macmillan & Co.

Holderness, Gale F. Ed. *East Africa (British): Its history, people, commerce, industries and resources,* (1908-9). Sommerset Playne, Comp. London, The Foreign and Colonial Compiling and Publishing Co.

Hollingsworth, L. W. *Asians in East Africa,* (1960), American Records, Salem Merchants.Rhodes House Library, Oxford, British Anti-Slavery Society, Rhodes.

Hollingsworth, M. G. *Asians in East Africa,* (1960), London, Macmillan.

Horton, M. C. and Bluston, T. R. *Indian Metalwork in East Africa: The Bronze Statuette from Shanga,* (1988). In Antiquity, 62.

Howe, Russel Warren. *Black Africa: Africa south of the Sahara from pre-history to Independence,* (1966), London, New African Library.

Howorth, David. *Dhows,* (1877), London: Quartet Books.

Huffman, T. N. *The Rise and Fall of Zimbabwe*, (1972). In JAH, vol. 13.

Huntingford, G. W. B. trans. *The Periplus of the Erythrean Sea*, (1980), London.

Hutchison, Edward. *The Slave Trade of East Africa,* (1970). Reprint of the 1874 ed. Allerthorpe, England, K Book Editions.
Huxley, Elspeth. *The Sorcerer's Apprentice,* (1949), London, Chatto and Windus.

Imperial Gazetteer of India, (The). *The Indian Empire of India, Vol. III*: Economic, (1908), Oxford, The Clarendon Press.

Indian Chamber of Commerce and Industry of Eastern Africa. Address by Mr. Kassam Lakha welcoming delegates to the 1st Session in Kisumu, July 1932. "The county's importance is economic not political . . . "

Indian National Association, Zanzibar. Address by Mr. Tayabali Esmailjee Jeevanjee. The Clove Industry Centenary 1843-1943.

Ingham, Kenneth. *A History of East Africa,* (1965). Rev. 1962 ed., New York, Praeger.

Ingrams, William H. *Arabia and the Isles,* (1966), London, John Murray.

Ingrams,William H. *Zanzibar: Its History and Peoples*, (1931), London, Wetherby.

Jackson, Frederick, Sir. *Early Days in East Africa,* (1969), London: Dawsons of Pall Mall.

Jaffe, Hosea. *A History of Africa, (1985),* London, Zed Books.

Jewell, John H. A. *Dhows at Mombasa,* (1969), Nairobi, East African Publishing House.

Jones, M. K. *The Slave Trade in Mauritius,* 1810-1829, (1936), Unpublished.

Josephy, Alvin M., et al. *The Horizon History of Africa,* (1971), New York, American Publishing Co.

July, R. W. *Pre-Colonial Africa,* (1976), Blanford, England.

July, Robert W. *A History of the African People*, (1970), London, Faber and Faber Limited.

Kenya Indian Congress. Presidential Address by N. S. Mangat, Q.C. 1954, see Mangat, N. S.

Kenya Indian Congress. Presidential Address by N. S. Mangat, Q.C. 1956, see Mangat, N. S.

Kesby, John D. *The Cultural Regions of East Africa,* (1977), London, Academic Press.

Khan, Z. M. *Politics of Regional Integration in East Africa,* (1985), English ed. Bombay, India: Advance Research Enterprise.

Khapoya, Vincent B. *The African Experience,* (1994), New Jersey, Prentice Hall.

Ki-Zerbo, J. Ed. *General History of Africa,* Vol. I, (1981). Methodology and Pre-History. California: UNESCO.

Kirk, W. The North-East Monsoon and Some Aspects of African History. (1962). In JAH, vol. 3, no. 2.

Kirkman, J. *The Early History of Oman in East Africa,* (1983), London. In Journal of *Oman Studies,* vol. 2.

Kirkman, James. *Fort Jesus: A Portuguese Fortress on the East African Coast,* (1974), Oxford, Clarendon Press.

Kirkman, J. *Men and Monuments on the East African Coast,* (1964), London, Lutterworth Press.

Kirkman, James. *Mombasa.* Mombasa: Friends of Fort Jesus, (1975).

Kotecha, Bhanuben. *On the Threshold of East Africa;* Translated from the original Gujerati by Lenore Reynell, (1994), London, Jyotiben Madhvani Foundation.

Kusimba, Chapuru Kha M. *The Rise and Fall of Swahili States,* (1999), New Delhi, Sage Publications.

Labouret, Henri. *Africa Before the White Man,* (1962), New York, Walker & Co.

Lamb, David. *The Africans,* New York, Random House.

Lanchester, H. V. Zanzibar: *A Study in Tropical Town Planning,* (1923), Cheltenham, Ed. J. Burrow & Co.

Langworthy, H. W. *Zambia Before 1890,* (1972), London.

Laufer, B. *The Giraffe in History and Art,* (1925), Chicago.

LeGuennec-Coppens, Francoise and Caplan, Patricia. *Les Swahili entre afrique et Arabie,* (1991), Paris, Karthala.

Lewick, T. *Arabic External Sources for Africa South of the Sahara,* (1974), London.

Lewis, A. *Maritime Skills in the Indian Ocean,* (1973). In JESHO, vol. 16.

Leys, Norman. *Kenya,* (1962), London, Leonard & Virginia Wolf at Hogarth Press.

Llyod, P. C. *Africa in Social Change,* Harmondsworth, Middlesex, England, Penguin Books.

Lodhi, Abdulaziz Y. et al. *A Small Book on Zanzibar,* (1979), Upsala, Forfattares Bokmaskin.

Lombard, D. and Aubin J. Eds. *Marchands et Chine 13e-20e siecles,* (1988), Paris.

Low, C. R. *History of the Indian Navy,* (1877), London.

Low, D. A. & Smith, Alison, Eds. *History of East Africa, vol. III.* (1976), Oxford, Clarendon Press.

Lugard, *F. D. Dairies,* (1959), 3 vols. Penham, M. and Bull, M. Eds., London.

Lugard, F. D. Sir. *The Dual Mandate in British Tropical Africa,* (1926), London, William Blackwood & Sons.

Lugard, F. D. *The Rise of Our East African Empire,* (1893), 2 vols., Edinburgh.

Lyne, Robert Nunez. *Zanzibar in Contemporary Times: A Short history of the southern east in the nineteenth century,* (1905), London, Hurst & Blackett.

Lytton, Noel Anthony. *The Stolen Desert: A Study in Uhuru in north east Africa,* London, Macdonald & Co.

Macmillan, Mona. *Introducing East Africa,* (1955). 2nd rev. ed., London, Faber and Faber.

Macmillan, W. M. *Africa Emergent,* (1949), London.

Macmillan's Magazine no.189, July 1875.

Mair, Lucy. (1962). *Primitive Government. Baltimore*: Penguin Books.

Maitland, A. *Speke*, (1971), London.

Major, R. H. *India in the Fifteenth Century,* (1957), London.

Mangat, J. S. *A History of the Asians in East Africa 1886 to 1945,* (1969), London, Oxford University Press.

Mangat, J. S. *The Immigrant Communities: The Asians in East Africa,* (1976), Nairobi.

Mangat, N. S. *The Kenya Indian Congress.* The Presidential Address by N. S. Mangat, Q. C. Delivered at the Twenty-Third Session on 31st July, 1st and 2nd August, 1954. Nairobi, Nairobi Printers.

Mangat, N. S. The Kenya Indian Congress. The Presidential Address by N. S. Mangat, Q. C. Delivered at the Twenty-Fourth Session at Nakuru on 4th, 5th and 6th August 1956. Nairobi, Nairobi Printers.

Mannick, A. R. Mauritius: *The Development of a plural society.* (1979), Nottingham.

Markovitz, Irving Leonard, Ed. *African Politics and Society,* (1970), New York, The Free Press.

Markovitz, Irving Leonard. *Power and Class in Africa,* (1977), New Jersey, Princeton-Hall.

Marsh, Zoe. *East Africa through Contemporary Records,* (1961), London, Cambridge University Press.

Marsh, Zoe and Kingsnorth, G. W. *An Introduction to the History of East Africa,* (1965), 3rd ed. Cambridge, England, Cambridge University Press.

Martin, E. B. and Martin, C. P. *Cargoes of the East,* (1987).

Mason, Philip. *Race Relations,* (1970). London, Oxford University Press.

Mas'udi, al. See al-Mas'udi.

McEwan, P. J. M. Ed. *Africa from Early Times to 1800,* (1968), London, Oxford University Press.

McGreggor Ross, *Kenya from Within: A short political history,* (1927), London, Allen & Unwin.

McKay, Vernon. *Africa in World Politics,* (1963), New York, Harper & Row Publishers.

Meister, Albert. *East Africa: The Past in chains, the future in pawn,* (1968), New York, Walker.

Middleton, John. *The Effects of Economic Development on Traditional Political Systems in Africa South of the Sahara,* (1966), The Hague, Mouton & Co.

Mielche, Hakon. *Zanzibar,* (1954), Copenhagen, Steen Hassela Lachs Forlag.

Mills, L. *Ceylon Under British Rule,* 1795-1932, (1933), Oxford.

Mishra, Vijay. *New Lamps for Old:* Diasporas, migrancy, borders.

Mitchison, Naomi. *The Africans,* (1970), London, Anthony Blond.

Mohamed, H. E. *The Asian Legacy in Africa and the White Man's Colour Culture,* (1979), New York, Vantage Press Inc.

Morris, H. S. *The Indians in Uganda,* (1968), London, Weidenfeld and Neilson.

Muller, Herbert J. *The Uses of the Past: A Mentor book,* (1951), New York, The New American Library.

Muloo, Anand Sawant. *Footprints,* (1968), Port Louis, Standard Printing Establishment.

Mungeam, G. H. *British Rule in Kenya,* 1895-1912, (1966), Oxford, Clarendon Press.

Murdock, George Peter. *Africa: Its Peoples and their culture history,* (1959), London, McGraw Hill Book Co.

Murphy, E. Jefferson. *History of African Civilization*, (1972), New York, Thomas Y. Cromwell Company.

Nambier, O.K. *The Kunjalis Admirals of Calicut*, (1963), London.

Nathoo, Ibrahim E. *Zanzibar: The Part Indians Have Played to Develop East Africa,* (1952), By Hon. Mr. Ibrahim E. Nathoo, Member of Legislative Council, Kenya, In The Samachar. Golden Jubilee number 1952. .

Nazareth, John Maximian. *Brown Man, Black Country,* (1981), New Delhi, Tidings Publications

Newitt, Malyn. *A History of Mozambique,* (1995), London, Hurst & Co.

Newitt, M. D. D. *Portuguese Settlement on the Zambezi*, (1973), London.

Nicholls, C. S. *The Swahili Coast: Politics, diplomacy and trade on the East African littoral, 1798-1856*, (1971), New York, Africana Pub. Corp.

Nurse, Derek & Spear, Thomas. *The Swahili: Restructuring the history and language of an African society, 800-1500,* (1985), Philadelphia, University of Pennsylvania Press.

Oliver, R. A. *The African Experience,* (1991), London.

Oliver, R. A. and Mathew, G. A. *A History of East Africa,* (1965), vol. I. Oxford.

Oliver, Roland and Fage, J. D. *A Short History of Africa,* (1962), Baltimore, MD, Penguin Books.

Oliver, Roland and Mathews, Gervase (1963). *History of East Africa, 2 vols.* London, Oxford University Press.

Osei, G. K. *Europe's Gift to Africa,* (1968), London, African Publication Society.

Owen, W. F. *Narrative of Voyages to Explore the Shores of Africa, Arabia and Madagascar, (1933), 2 vols,* London.

Padmore, George (MCMXLIX). *Africa: Britain's Third Empire,* London, Dennis Dobson.

Palgrave, William Gifford. *Narrative of a Year's Journey Through Central and Eastern Africa, 1862-63, vol. II. (1865)*, London, Macmillan & Co.

Pandurang, Mala. *Boundaries and Belonging: A Socio-literary investigation of East African Asian diasporic experience*. Project submitted under the INDAL Fellowship for Social Sciences, Bombay, Asiatic Society of Bombay.

Panikkar, K. M. *Asia and Western Dominance*, (1953), London.

Panikkar, K. M. *Malabar and the Portuguese,* (1929), Bombay.

Parry, J. H. *The Discovery of the Sea,* (1975), London.

Patel, Zarina. *Challenge to Colonialism: The Struggle of Alibhai Mulla Jeevanjee for Equal Rights in Kenya,* (1997), Nairobi, Zand Graphics.

Pearce, F. B. Zanzibar, the Island Metropolis of East Africa, (1920), London.

Pearson, Michael N. Port Cities and Intruders: *The Swahili coast, India and Portugal in the early modern era,* (1998), Baltimore, MD, Johns Hopkins University Press.

Pearson, M. N. *The Portuguese in India,* (1987). In New Cambridge History of India, vol. I. Cambridge.

Pennington, L. E. Hakluytus Posthumus: *Samuel Purchas and the promotion of English overseas expansion,* (1966), Kansas, Emporia.
Perham, M. and Simons, J. *African Discovery,* (1961), London.

Perham, M. *The Colonial Reckoning,* (1956), London.

Pescatello, A. M. *The African Presence in Portuguese India,* (1977). In Journal of African History, vol. II.

Phillipson, D. W. *African Archeology,* (1985), London.

Pieris, P. E. *Some Documents Relating to the Rise of Dutch Power in Ceylon.* Colombo, (1929).

Pirès Tomé. *Trade Relations of the East Coast with Europe, Arabia and the Far East, 1512-1515.* Written in Malacca where he retired c1512-1514, Trans. by Armando Cortesco for the Hakluyt Society.

Playne, Sommerset, Comp. See Holderness, Gale F. Ed.

Posnansky, Merrick, Ed. *Prelude to East African History*: A Collection of papers, (1966), London, Oxford University Press.

Pradhan, K. K. See E*ast Africa Indian National Congress.* 13th Session.

Prasad, R. C. *Early English Travellers in India,* (1980), Delhi.

Prestage, E. *The Portuguese Pioneers,* (1933), London.

Prior, J. *Voyage along the Eastern Coast of Africa in the Nexus Frigate,* (1819), London.

Pruen, S. Tristram. *The Arab and the African*: Experiences in eastern Equatorial Africa during a residence of three years, (1891), London, Seely and Co. Ltd.

Patak, R. *China and Calicut in the Early Ming Period,* (1989). In JRAS, no. 1.

Qaisar, A. J. *The Indian Resopnse to European Technology and Culture, 1498-1707,*Delhi

Ramachandani, R. R. Ed. *India and Africa,* (1980), New Delhi, Radiant Publishers Ltd.

Ramanathan, P. *The Ethnology of the Moors of Ceylon,* (1988). In JRAS, vol. 10. Ceylon.

Ranger, T. O. Ed. *Aspects of Central African History,* (1968), London.

Ravensworth, E. G. trans. *Unknown Journal of the First Voyage of Vasco da Gama,* (1899). Translated for the Hakluyt Society.

Ravestein, E. G. Ed. *A Journal of the First Voyage of Vasco da Gama,* (1988), London.

Ravichandra, Annapoorna. *Negotiations which led to the British Protectorate (1824-1826), (1989),* Vol. 1, Lisboa, Ministerio da Educacao, Instituto de Investigardo Cientifica Tropical. In Stvdia, see also Stvdia

Report on the Zanzibar Dominions by Lt. Col. C. P. Rigby, B*ombay Army, H.M. Consul and British Agent in Zanzibar.* Signed by British Consul in Zanzibar, 1st July 1860, (1861). In Selections from the Records of the Bombay Government No. LIX. Bombay: Bombay Educational Security Press.

Reusch, Richard. *History of East Africa.* (1954), Stuttgart, Evang. Missions, Verlag.

Reusch, Richard. *History of East Africa,* (1961), New York, F. Ungar Pub. Co.

Rey, C. F. *The Romance of the Portuguese in Abyssinia,* (1929), London.

Reynolds, C. G. *Command of the Sea,* (1974), New York.

Richards, Audrey I. *The Multicultural States of East Africa,* (1969), Montreal, Published for the Centre by McGill-Queen's University Press.

Richards, Charles G. and Place, James. *East African Explorers.* Nairobi, Oxford University Press.

Ricks, T. C. *Persian Gulf Seafaring and East Africa,* (1970). In African Historical Studies, vol.3, no. 2.

Rigby, Christopher Palmer, Lt. Col. Selections from the Records of the Bombay Government No. LIX, (1861). Report on the Zanzibar Dominions by Lt. Col. C. P. Rigby, Bombay Army and H.M. Consul and British Agent at Zanzibar. Signed July 1860. Educational Society Press. [Settlers from India].

Ritner, Peter. *The Death of Africa,* (1960), New York, Macmillan Company.

Roberts, *A. Pre-Colonial Trade in Zambia.* (1970). In African Social Research, vol. 10.

Roberts, Andrew. Recording *East Africa's Past: A Brief guide for the amateur historian,* (1968), Nairobi, East African Publishing House.

Roberts, Andrew. *Safari: Records of East Africa's past,* (1971), Lusaka, Zambia, Oxford University Press.

Robertson, W. *An Historical Disquisition Concerning the Knowledge the Ancients had of India,* (1971), Edinburg.

Rodwell, Edward. *Coast Causerie: Stories of the coast and beyond,* (1972), Nairobi, Heinemann Educational Books.

Rosenthal, F. *A Fourteenth Century Report on Ethiopia,* (1983). In Ethiopian Studies. Weisbaden.

Rossed, R. *The Dutch on the Swahili Coast, 1776-1778,* (1986). In International Journal of African Historical Studies, vol. 5, nos. 2, 3.

Ruchchenberger, W. S. *Narrative of a Voyage Round the World During the Years 1835, 1836 and 1837,* (1838). vol. I. London.

Russel, Charles A.B. (Mrs) Ed. General Rigby, *Zanzibar and the Slave Trade,* (1935). Reprint of the 1935 Edition, New York, Negro Universities Press.

Said-Ruete, Rudolph. *Said bin Sultan, (1791-1856), Ruler of Oman: His place in the history of Arabia and East Africa,* (1971), London, Alexander-Ousley Ltd.

Sakarai, Lawerence J. *Indian Merchants in East Africa: Part II.* British Imperialim and the Transformation of the Slave Economy, (1981). In Journal of Slavery and Abolition, v. 2, 1881, University of Bombay.

Saloni, Deepalsingh and Carter, Marina. (1996), *Select Documents on Indian Immigration.* Mauritius 1834-1926, Vol. III: Living and Working Under Indenture. Moka: Mahatma Gandhi Institute.

Salvadori, Cynthia. *Through Open Doors: A View of Asian cultures in Kenya,* (rev. 1989), Nairobi, Kenway.

Salvadori, Cynthia. *Two Indian Travellers: East Africa 1903-1905,* (1997). Being accounts of journeys made by Ebrahim N. Adamji, a very young Bohora merchant, & Sorabji M. Darukhanawala, a middle-aged Parsi Engineer from Zanzibar. Mombasa, Friends of Fort Jesus.

Salvadori, Cynthia. *We Came in Dhows,* (1996), Nairobi, Paperchase Kenya Ltd.

Samachar, (The) *Golden Jubilee Number,* 1952, see Nathoo, Ibrahim E.

Samachar, (The) *Silver Jubilee Number*, 1929, Chronicles of the Indian Societies in Zanzibar.

Samson, Ombongi Kenneth. *Hindu Socio-Religious Organizations in Kenya,* (1993). Thesis submitted in partial fulfilment of the degree of Master of Arts in the University of Nairobi.

Seidenberg, Dana April. *Mercantile Adventurers: The World of East African Asians,* 1750-1985, (1996), New Delhi, New Age International (P) Ltd., Publishers.

Seidenberg, Dana April. *Uhuru and the Kenya Asian,* (1983), New Delhi, Vikas Publishing House.

Sharif, Abdul and Fergusson, Ed. *Zanzibar Under Colonial Rule,* (1991), London, James Curry.

Sharma, Vishva B. L. *Developing Societies: Africa and Asia,* Denver, Colorado, Morton Publishing Company.

Sharma, Vishva B. L. *Pubjabi and Gujerati Immigrants in East Africa*: A Comparative study. (1989). In The 8th Annual Conference on South Asia, Madison, Wisconson.

Shboul, A. *Al-Masudi and His World,* (1979), London.

Shepherd, G. *The Making of the Swahili,* (1982). In Paideuma, 28.

Sheriff, *A. Ivory and Commercial Expansion in East Africa in the Nineteenth Century.* (1983). From Proceedings of the Symposium on Qualification and Structure of the Import and Export and Long Distance Trade of the 19th Century (1800-1913). St. Augustin 3-6 January 1986.

Sheriff, Abdul & Curry, James, Eds. (1991). *The Formation of a Colonial Economy,* 1915-1945. In Zanzibar Under Colonial Rule. London: James Curry.

Sheriff, Abdul and Curry, James. *Slaves, Spices and Ivory in Zanzibar: Integration of the East African Commercial Empire into the World Economy, 1770-1873,* (1987), London, James Curry.

Shillington, Kevin. *History of Africa,* (1989), London, Macmillan.

Silver Jubilee Number, December 1836. *Indians in Zanzibar*: Commenting on the reign of H. M. The Sultan Seyyid Sir Khalifa bin Harub.

South and East Africa Yearbook & Guide,1948.

Spear, T. *Kenya's Past,* (1981).

Speke, John Hannington. *Journal of the Discovery of the Source of the Nile,* (1863), Edinburg, London.

Stanley, Henry Morton. How I Found Livingstone, (1872), London.

Stigand, C. H. The Land of Zinj, (1966), London, Frank Cass & Co. Ltd.

Stigand, C. H. *The Land of Zinj*: Being an account of British East Africa, its ancient history and present inhabitants, (1913), London, Constable & Company.

Strandes, Justus. *The Portuguese Period in East Africa,* (1961). Translated from the German by Jean F. Wallwork. Edited by J. S. Kirkman. Nairobi, East African Literature Bureau.

Strandes, Justus. *The Portuguese Period in East Africa.* (1968). 2nd ed. Nairobi, East African Literature Bureau.

Strayer, Robert W., Steinhart, Edward I. and Maxon, Robert M. *Protest Movements in Colonial East Africa:* Aspects of early African response to European rule, (1973), Syracuse, NY, Program of Eastern African Studies, Syracuse University.

Strong, S. A. Ed. *The History of Kilwa,* (1995). In JRAS, vol. 20.

Stvdia. *Vol. I, Negotiations Which Led to the British Protectorate (1824-1826),* (1989). By Annapoorna Ravichandra. Vol. 2, Indian Textiles and the Portuguese Trade in the 17th Century (1600-1663), By Afzal Ahmad. Lisboa, Ministerio da Educacao, Instituto de Investigado Cientifica Tropical.
Sulivan, George Lydiard. *Dhow Chasing in Zanzibar Waters and on the Eastern Coast of Africa:* Narrative of five years' experiences in the suppression of the slave trade, (1967), London, Dawsons of the Pall Mall. Originally Published 1873. London: Royal Navy.

Sutton, John E. G. *The East African Coast: An Historical and archeological review.* Nairobi, East African Publishing House.

Sutton, J. E. G. *The East African Coast: An Historical and archeological review,* (1966). In Historical Association of Tanzania, Paper, no. 1, Nairobi, East African Publishing House.

Sutton, John E. G. *A Thousand Years of East Africa,* (1990), Nairobi, British Institute in Eastern Africa.

Swai, Bonaventure. *Pre-Colonial States and European Merchant Capital in Eastern Africa,* (1979), Dar es Salaam, University of Dar es Salaam.

Taylor, Robert, Capt. (1856). *Extracts from Brief Notes Containing Historical and Other Information Connected with the Province of Oman , Muscat and the Adjoining Countries.* Prepared by Capt. Robert Taylor in 1818. Printed by Bombay Educational Society's Press, 1856.

Thorbhan, P. F. *The Pre-Colonial Ivory Trade of East Africa,* Cambridge Mass. Unpublished Manuscript.

Tolmacheva, M. *Towards a Definition of the Term Zanj,* (1986). In Azania, vol. 21.

Trimzi, S. A. L. Ed. *Indian Sources for African History,* (1988). Vol. I, Delhi, International Emporium.

Tucker, A. R. *Eighteen Years in Uganda and East Africa,* (1908), London, Edward Arnold.

UNESCO. *Historical Relations Across the Indian Ocean*: Report and papers of the Meeting of Experts organized by Unesco at Port Louis, Mauritius from 15 to 19 July 1974, (1980), Paris, Unesco.

Vaghella, B. G. Ed. *East Africa Today 1958-1959*: A Comprehensive directory of British East Africa with Who's Who, Bombay, Overseas Information Publishers.

Verin, P. *The African Element in Madagascar,* (1976). In Azania, vol. 11.

Visram, M. G. *The Trail Blazer.* (1990), Mombasa.

Waines, David Ed. *The Revolt of the Zanj,* (1992), New York.

Were, G. S. and Wilson, D. A. *East Africa Through a Thousand Years,* (1986), London, Evans Brothers Ltd.

Wiedner, Donald L. *A History of Africa South of the Sahara.* New York, Random House.

Wilkinson, J. C. *Oman and East Africa: New light on early Kilwan history from Oman sources,* (1981). In Journal of African Historical Studies, vol. 14, no. 2.

Wraith, Ronald E. *East African Citizen,* (1959), London, Oxford University Press.

Zanzibar a Commercial Power. In Macmillan Magazine, no.198, July 1875.

INDEX

A

B

C

D

E